"This book does what it promises—walks us through the steps it will take to lo͟v̶ particularly moved by the exercises. They not only show us where our work is, bu͟t a toolkit for skillful relating. Best of all, it is written with great compassion for al̶. ͟are still trying to get relating right."

—**David Richo, PhD**, author of *How to Be an Adult in Relationships*

"*The Insecure in Love Workbook* is a practical, compassionate guide that gives a clear pathway forward out of an anxious attachment style and into greater self-love and relational security."

—**Eli Harwood**, author of *Securely Attached*

"Following the excellence of *Insecure in Love*, this workbook is a highly recommended next step to put the amazing and deep insights of the text into practice. Anyone looking to live in a secure love relationship will be wisely guided along the path. We recommend it for everyone."

—**Harville Hendrix, PhD**, and **Helen LaKelly Hunt, PhD**, coauthors of *Getting the Love You Want*

"Close relationships are the source of our great joys, but also great pains and grief. The wide-ranging insight from this book expertly guides readers through some of the processes underpinning our ability to form and nurture close relationships (attachments), and how to develop insight into how our minds function when in relationships. Bringing together many different strands from different therapies, such as cognitive behavior therapy (CBT), mindfulness, mentalizing, and others, Becker-Phelps offers multiple ways we can come to understand ourselves and develop our capacity for working with the ups-and-downs and complexities of close relationships. This is a marvelous resource for those wanting to explore their own relating style and how to improve it."

—**Paul Gilbert, PhD, FBPsS, OBE**, professor of clinical psychology at the University of Derby (UK); visiting professor at the University of Queensland, Australia; and author *of The Compassionate Mind* and *Living Like Crazy*

"This transformative workbook, with the compassionate guidance of Becker-Phelps, will result in increased self-awareness and self-love. Improving your relationship with yourself will prepare and enable you to have the healthy love relationship that you desire and deserve. *The Insecure in Love Workbook* is an essential guide for anyone longing for love."

—**Michelle Skeen, PsyD**, author of several self-help books, including *Love Me, Don't Leave Me* and *Why Can't I Let You Go?*

The
Insecure
in Love
Workbook

Step-by-Step Guidance to Help You Overcome Anxious
Attachment & Feel More Secure with Yourself & Your Partner

Leslie Becker-Phelps, PhD

New Harbinger Publications, Inc.

Publisher's Note

NEW HARBINGER PUBLICATIONS is a registered trademark of New Harbinger Publications, Inc.

New Harbinger Publications is an employee-owned company.

Copyright © 2024 by Leslie Becker-Phelps
New Harbinger Publications, Inc.
5720 Shattuck Avenue
Oakland, CA 94609
www.newharbinger.com

Cover design by Sara Christian

Acquired by Jennye Garibaldi

Edited by Brady Kahn

Printed in the United States of America

26   25   24

10   9   8   7   6   5   4   3   2   1   First Printing

Imperfectly Perfect

We are all imperfect.
But none broken.
You may feel down to your bones
deep in your soul
BROKEN
Or INFERIOR
but you are NOT
broken
Or inferior.
You are not a toaster or
A wrench or a car
To be rated
Superior or inferior.
To break from use
or imperfect parts
or faulty assembly.
You are a person,
A sentient being.
Your body can break.
Your bones,
Even your nose.
But you, your inherent
True, AUTHENTIC
SELF
Cannot break.
It can ache

Or rage
Or be nauseatingly filled with pain.
You can hurt to your core.
But despite how it feels,
You are NOT broken,
But HURTING.
Pain cannot be fixed.
Only healed.
Your being requires
Light and
Warmth and
Love—
A quickening of healing
for the shards of brokenness you feel
piercing your very being,
but that being,
Your AUTHENTIC self,
is *unbroken.*
It is whole—
Hurting,
Perhaps excruciatingly so,
But still whole
And worthy
And as lovable as the setting sun
Over a turbulent ocean filled with awe-inspiring life.

Contents

Foreword

We all want to feel loving and loved. It's literally encoded into our DNA, and we evolved to need cooperation and love, in order to function as a species. Humans have evolutionary advantages that are rooted in our ability to work together, not in our ability to be some super-deadly, wildly individual apex predator like a lion or cobra. Cooperating to survive, hunting together, communicating using words, thinking using internalized language, and protecting and nurturing one another are what has brought dominance on the planet.

We are a species that needs love, and that fact will seriously affect any member of this species for their entire time on earth. Indeed, your experience of loving relationships and caring connection is an essential element of your own survival and flourishing. Research from across a range of scientific disciplines suggests that, from the day you are born until the day you die, your experience of compassion and love will affect your health at every level of well-being from your immune system to your heart rate variability to your resilience in the face of adversity and psychological stress.

Given all of this, why is it that finding and nurturing a loving relationship can be so desperately challenging? And, why is it that when we show others our basic human need to feel safe and loved, we fear seeming "needy" or "insecure"? It's almost as if modern society encourages us to be ashamed of our needs, ashamed of what makes us most human, and ashamed of who we are. How can we come to understand the dynamics of human relationships?

"Attachment," a word from psychological science that can be defined as our enduring connectedness with emotionally significant others across time and situations, has become something of a buzzword in the 2020s. Social media and pop psychology have brought "attachment" into the zeitgeist, with a seemingly endless stream of mental health influencers posting videos to your social media feed. These posts and reels might talk about your "attachment style," or offer platitudes that can define and categorize your "attachment style," putting your way of loving and relating into a kind of box, with yet another new label. You can be trained to think of yourself as "anxiously attached" or "insecure" without really absorbing information that can guide effective action in the world. This isn't so helpful. In a sense, it resembles astrology, where your whole being can be reduced to a zodiac sign based on very little data (your birth date in that case), without you really receiving actionable intelligence about how to live. Maybe you don't need a new label so much. Maybe you need a map to the road ahead, and a friendly voice that teaches you how to reclaim your life, and to build opportunities for love to flourish in your life.

In this workbook, you will learn that the science of attachment, love, and compassion isn't meant to function like a horoscope or label. The cutting edge of clinical attachment science is meant to help you transform your life and walk forward on a loving and empowered path. This workbook will show you that finding love doesn't need to be a grueling and shameful endeavor. The author provides practical steps to work with your fundamental need for human connection in ways that can help you discover love, within and without. As you will soon discover, Dr. Becker-Phelps can gradually and kindly guide you as you learn how to love yourself, learn how to overcome psychological blocks to being available to love, and learn how to build meaningful and rewarding relationships that have the possibility of enduring and thriving.

I hope that you find the love that you desire and need. I hope that you learn to accept yourself exactly as you are in this very moment. Finding that love within, beginning to share a gently accepting, nonjudgmental love with yourself, can change everything. I'm glad you have found this book, and I wish you well as you begin this journey with the author. May you be well.

—Dr. Dennis Tirch

Acknowledgments

This workbook is essentially a response to the many people who have read *Insecure in Love*. While I have been gratified to hear from readers about how *Insecure in Love* has helped them on their paths of healing, it was my editor, Jennye Garibaldi, who suggested that I create a workbook to offer further guidance, and who helped me through the process of making this idea a reality.

Rather than thinking of this workbook as *my baby*, I think of myself as its midwife. I have integrated the ideas, theories, research, and teachings of those who have worked to understand and help people struggling with insecure attachment. There is no way to list all of my influences, but I am especially indebted to John Bowlby and Mary Ainsworth, who gave breath to attachment theory. Still, they are only part of a larger unfolding history in psychology, and I am grateful to *all* those who have influenced this ever-growing human endeavor to facilitate healing. (You can see some of them by looking at this book's list of references.)

In a very real way, lessons from my patients have also shaped how I have come to think about people's insecurity and my journey in learning how to best help them. These lessons are very much at the heart of this workbook. So, to all of you who have allowed me to accompany you on your personal journey, thank you.

Finally, I greatly appreciate the input and guidance of my editors. As always, at the top of this list is my unofficial editor and chief supporter, my husband, Mark Phelps.

Introduction

You feel more than ready to be in a happy, committed relationship. Unfortunately, your attempts at dating have not worked out so well, leaving you with the question of what to do next. This workbook might be just what you are looking for. It offers guidance in how to nurture the relationship you've always wanted.

Even if you haven't read my book *Insecure in Love*, this workbook will show you how a well-researched conception of the human attachment system—attachment theory—can help you understand the biological foundation of how you connect with significant others. A fundamental idea from this theory is that the way you relate to others is based on how lovable you feel and on how emotionally available you tend to think others will be. This workbook frequently uses this idea and other concepts in attachment theory to help you think about how the patterns in your relationships have developed, how you maintain them, and how you can change them. Given that my previous books, *Insecure in Love* and *Bouncing Back from Rejection*, were both based on the same fundamental concepts, I have used them as resources in developing the current workbook.

While your goal is to be happy in a love relationship, it is essential that you begin by focusing on yourself and what you bring to relationships. If you feel flawed or broken, you will undoubtedly feel anxious and insecure in the presence of a potential partner. In the past, convinced that no one who really got to know you would want to be your partner, you may have worked hard to "make" people happy. Or to convince people to love you. After all, it's hard, if not impossible, for you to imagine someone loving the real you (the true you, not your façade).

So, you must begin your journey toward being secure in love by learning to be *at home* within yourself. But how can you feel at home if you are already caught up in being critical of yourself and fearing judgment? The answer is to learn to relate to yourself as a being who is struggling rather than as an object that needs to be taken apart, scrutinized, and fixed. You must learn to more fully see and have empathy and compassion for your true self—including the unwelcome pull to be self-critical. With this *compassionate self-awareness*, you will begin to heal your inner insecurity. But there is still the matter of wanting to feel more secure in a relationship with another person.

With increased compassionate self-awareness and self-acceptance, you will be more open to feeling accepted and cared about by someone else. Then, as you absorb their positive responses, your inner self will feel more secure…and you will become even more open to caring from another. And so it goes, with each of these experiences feeding the other, and your sense of security in yourself and your relationship increasing. This personal growth will enable you to be more empathic, compassionate, supportive, and encouraging of your partner, all of which are essential for a happy, loving relationship.

Tips for Using This Workbook

The *Insecure in Love Workbook* is a step-by-step guide to renewing your inner home. There will be exercises to do throughout this workbook, and some free tools and bonus content are also available at https://drbecker-phelps.com/insecure-in-love-workbook and http://www.newharbinger.com/52175. There is so much to learn about yourself and your relationships that I strongly suggest journaling to process thoughts, questions, concerns, observations, and insights stirred up by this workbook. Although there are certain times when I will encourage you to write in the journal, I also encourage you to do this at any point when you think it would be helpful.

Keep in mind that you don't need to be alone in this journey. And ultimately, you *cannot* do it alone, because your goal is to nurture a secure romantic relationship. You may find it helpful to get feedback along the way from someone else, such as a friend or a therapist. You can also use the exercises in this workbook to develop greater security in platonic relationships as a way to prepare for having a romantic partner.

As you nurture a sense of feeling truly secure within yourself and become more open to being loved by another, you will finally be able to create a shared home, a relationship in which you and a partner can safely reside and even thrive.

CHAPTER 1

A Blueprint for Love

You may question what's wrong with you that makes it so hard to enjoy a healthy, loving, intimate relationship. This sense of being fundamentally flawed can be deeply painful, even torturous. So, I'm hoping you will find it a relief to learn that there is nothing inherently wrong with you as a person. Rather, your struggles are related to being human...and even more broadly, to just being a mammal. Once you understand this, you will see that you are not deficient, and you are not alone. Like other people, you can enjoy fulfilling, intimate relationships. But to get there, it can help to first learn about how your human capacity for close relationships has been misdirected. (*You may be shaking your head, unconvinced that you are not the problem. But stay with me. This workbook will help you see the truth in what I'm proposing here.*)

Though we humans like to focus on how our complex, neuron-packed brains make us special, and despite all of the "progress" we've made as a species, our ability to survive is based on neural wiring shared with other mammals: *the need right from birth to connect with others in our species.* This need is also the foundation of love relationships, which provide a home for our hearts.

You have an intrinsic appreciation of this when you see all those mother-baby animal pictures passed along through the internet, leaving us to practically sigh together in a collective "Awww!" Mammals can also feel this connection across species. Think about how you feel when you see those pictures of kittens and puppies playing together. *They're so darned cute!*

Psychoanalyst John Bowlby (1969) developed and explored this wired-in need for connection in his concept of *attachment theory.* As infants, we clearly need caregivers to attend to us and keep us safe. However, on a less obvious level, the role of those caregivers is to comfort us, though our personal temperament and physiology can make this more or less difficult to accomplish. The more successful they are in creating a physically and emotionally safe environment, the less anxiety we feel within ourselves and the better we become at managing perceived threats. We also learn to see our caregivers as emotionally available resources that we can turn to for support. However, when people don't feel valued and supported, they develop negative self-perceptions, have difficulty managing their emotions, and may have difficulty developing healthy relationships. These are lessons we carry into adulthood.

The relationship that children have with their caregivers—what Bowlby calls *attachment figures*—shapes their lifelong relationship with themselves and others. The researchers Bartholomew and Horowitz (1991) referred to these lifelong relationships as the *model of self* and *model of others.* Later we will use these models to explore the four basic *attachment styles.*

Model of Self

A person's model of self is characterized by how worthy or lovable they feel. It is largely developed from their experiences of being attended to by caregivers, especially in their first several years.

There are two basic ways in which children develop a sense that they are worthy. The healthiest grounding comes when caregivers tend to be emotionally attuned to a child and respond in a compassionate and calming way. These caregivers, or attachment figures, can include parents, teachers, and mentors. By taking in their nurturing, a child also absorbs the message that they are essentially lovable and have value in just being (not solely for what they do). So, in the face of upsetting emotions, they can self-soothe by effectively replicating the responses of their caregivers, rather than becoming easily overwhelmed or questioning themselves. Overall, they develop a positive, accepting relationship with themselves and feel comfortable in their own skin.

Another way that people achieve feeling worthy is by overriding their distress and focusing on the external world. They feel worthy and valuable based on what they can accomplish without looking to an attachment figure. They also experience themselves as lovable based on their sense of accomplishment. (It will become clear later that this way of developing a positive sense of self has its downsides.)

However, other children develop a sense that they are unworthy. There are many children who feel outright rejected or do not feel sufficiently comforted when upset. They receive the message that there is something essentially wrong with them. Unable to effectively be calmed by others or themselves, they often feel some degree of being unsafe in the world or in relationships. Feeling distressed or "bad" can lead them to see themselves as "bad," or in ways akin to being inadequate, unworthy, and unlovable. They can sometimes attain an illusory sense of being worthy by eliciting reassurance from others, but this is fragile and easily gives way to the underlying sense that there is something wrong with them. Feelings of anxiety within themselves and their relationships reflect their *anxious attachment style*.

Exploring Your Model of Self

It is important to understand that the model of self is a dimension, or range. Everyone has good and bad days, but people generally feel a greater or lesser sense of being lovable and calm or unlovable and anxious. If you tend to experience yourself in the latter way, you have a more anxious attachment style.

To determine your model of self and your level of anxious attachment, read over these contrasting perceptions that people can have of themselves. Then place a tick mark on the lines to show where in these ranges, on a day-to-day, general basis, your perceptions of yourself fall. The far right of the scales correlates to an anxious attachment style.

Lovable _____ Unlovable

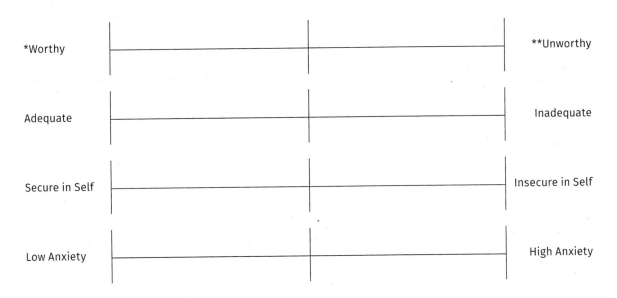

*Worthy			**Unworthy
Adequate			Inadequate
Secure in Self			Insecure in Self
Low Anxiety			High Anxiety

*Worthy: sound, strong, acceptable
**Unworthy: flawed, inferior, weak, deficient

Reflect on your model-of-self profile from this assessment. Can you think of some recent experiences that support your responses? If these experiences go back to childhood, describe the earliest examples of them that you can remember. What patterns do you notice in these scales? If your experiences of self are different now from when you were a child, how have they changed? Do your responses differ for different kinds of relationships? Have they changed over time?

_____

_____

_____

_____

_____

_____

_____

Do you have more to explore? If so, continue writing in your journal.

Is Your Model of Self Making You Anxious?

Look at your ratings in the last exercise. If they reflect an anxious attachment style, your responses show that you relate to yourself as a flawed or deficient person. As you consider the following ways in which such a negative self-relationship is often expressed, check off any that you believe apply to you:

Within Yourself

☐ Feeling insecure, dependent, weak, inferior, flawed, or inadequate

☐ Feeling not as good or as competent as other people in your life

☐ Feeling alone in the world (even when others are around or supportive)

☐ Being self-critical (which can also be self-bullying)

☐ Feeling shame, self-loathing

☐ Being angry with yourself for your perceived flaws

☐ Withdrawing into yourself in response to feeling so negatively about yourself

☐ Fearing being overwhelmed by your emotions

☐ Believing intense emotions show that there is something wrong with you

Self in Relation to Others

☐ Being quick to see others as rejecting you

☐ Fearing rejection or abandonment

☐ Withdrawing from others to avoid rejection

☐ Being angry with others for not being as available or supportive as you feel you need or for not somehow making you feel better

☐ Trying desperately to prove to others that you are worthy or to gain their support

☐ Being needy or clingy

Reflect on each phrase that you checked. The more you relate to these phrases, the more anxiously attached you are. Which phrases do you connect with most powerfully? Think of situations that relate to the different phrases. Do you notice patterns in how or when you have these experiences? How do the phrases that you checked off in the "Within Yourself" section relate to the ones that you checked off in the "Self in Relation to Others" section? How might your life be improved by addressing these issues?

_____

_____

_____

_____

_____

_____

_____

_____

If you have more to say, continue writing in your journal.

As you work to create a more positive self-relationship, you will notice that you have fewer of the experiences that you noted in the previous exercise and feel less intensely about the ones you do have.

Model of Others

A person's model of others (particularly of attachment figures) during times of distress can range from seeing them as emotionally available to seeing them as unavailable or even hostile. As with the model of self, the model of others is largely developed from early experiences with caregivers. Children who experience others as emotionally available have also experienced their caregivers as emotionally available, caring, and capable of calming their distress.

The story is different for children who experience their caregivers as uncaring, too weak or flawed to help, or as hostile. They expect that turning to these caregivers during times of distress will be harmful, either leaving them painfully vulnerable and alone or on the receiving end of harsh treatment. To cope with this, they essentially try to turn off their attachment system by denying or suppressing their distress, thus not needing to connect with an attachment figure. They focus outwardly on mastering their environment, such as by playing with their toys, achieving success at school, and, later as adults, being successful in their chosen careers. To the degree that they are externally successful, they view themselves positively. They are inclined to avoid their own emotional experiences as well as emotional closeness with others, and so they are said to have an *avoidant attachment style*.

Exploring Your Model of Others

To assess how emotionally available you expect significant people in your life to be, and how open you are to emotional intimacy, consider these ranges of experience. Place a tick mark on each line to show where in these ranges your perceptions of, and reactions to, attachment figures fall. Though your experiences may vary, respond based on what you generally experience on a day-to-day basis. If your expectations differ between family, platonic, and romantic relationships, you may want to mark them separately (perhaps using a different color pen.)

You expect others are emotionally available			You expect others are emotionally unavailable

You tend not to avoid others			You tend to avoid others
You approach others for support			You do not approach others for support
You expect others will not reject you			You expect others will reject you

Though the right side of these scales indicates characteristics of a more avoidant attachment style, the first scale can be a little different. Many anxiously attached people think that others can be emotionally available, but they also think they don't deserve such acceptance and love unless they work hard to earn it. If you can relate to this, you likely have anxious attachment style despite possibly placing your tick mark to the right of center.

Reflect on your model-of-others profile from this assessment. What are some recent examples of experiences that support your responses? If these experiences go back to childhood, describe the earliest examples that you can remember. What patterns do you notice in these scales? If your experiences of others are different now from when you were a child, how have they changed? Do your responses differ with different kinds of relationships? Have they changed over time?

_____

_____

_____

_____

_____

_____

Do you have more to explore? If so, continue writing in your journal.

Is Your Model of Others Making You Avoidant?

Consider the following ways in which you might avoid closeness with others. Check off each one that you believe applies to you.

Self in Relation to Others

☐ Independent

☐ Self-sufficient

☐ Relatively uninterested in others' personal matters

Your Perception of Others

☐ Unreliable or incompetent

☐ Unsupportive

☐ Uncaring

☐ Untrustworthy

☐ Rejecting

☐ Critical

☐ Not emotionally available or supportive in general

☐ Emotionally available and supportive, but not to you unless you earn it

Reflect on your responses to this exercise. The more you think of others as failing to be emotionally available *for anyone*, the more likely you tend toward being avoidantly attached. The last couple of items are particularly revealing. If you checked the very last one, you have a model of self in which you feel flawed, likely reflecting an anxious attachment style. In this case, you probably feel driven to prove your worth to earn others' caring and support. If, instead, you checked the preceding box, about others not being emotionally available in general, then you probably checked a number of the other boxes, reflecting that you likely have an avoidant style. Finally, if you checked off both of them, your attachment style may be conflicted, with you having traits of both anxious and avoidant styles.

Explore your model of others by reflecting on your responses and answering these questions. If you endorse a number of the statements above, do you also notice that you tend to feel that you're on your own? How willing are you to reach out for, or to accept, support? What is your reaction to the thought of accepting support from others whom you are close to? Record your thoughts here.

_____

_____

_____

_____

_____

_____

_____

_____

_____

_____

If you have more to say, continue writing in your journal.

By gaining a better understanding of your model of others, you will develop greater insight into your relationships and potentially see how you can improve them.

Understanding the Four Attachment Styles

Using the models of self and others, you have learned about two broad styles of insecure attachment—anxious and avoidant—but there are actually four specific attachment styles. We can understand all of these styles by combining the model of self and model of others in the graph in figure 1.

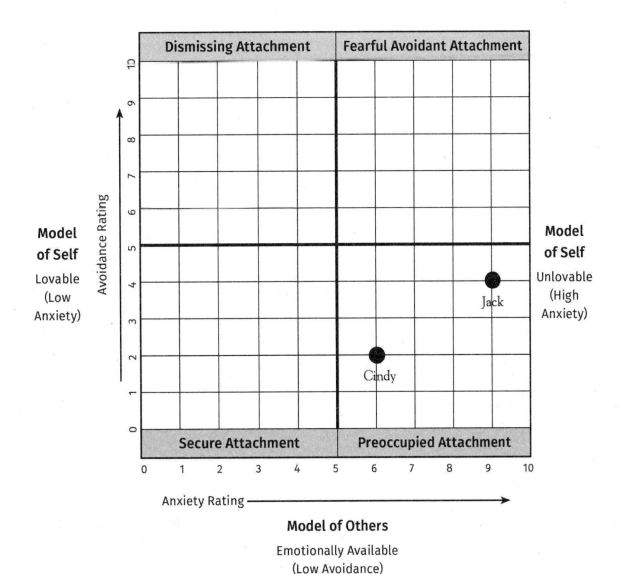

Figure 1

Though there are four different attachment styles, it is important to understand that these are loose categories because each point on the graph is different. The figure includes Cindy and Jack as examples. As you can see, both have a preoccupied attachment style, but Cindy feels more positively about herself than Jack does, and she also sees others as more emotionally available. Similarly, as you identify your attachment style, it's important to recognize that there is much more to understand about what is going on for you. Also, as mentioned earlier, you can operate from different attachment styles in different relationships, and at different times in your life.

With this in mind, let's turn our attention to learning more about the four attachment styles, of which only one is a secure style.

Secure Attachment

People with a secure attachment style feel positively about themselves and expect that significant others will be emotionally available, especially at times when they are distressed. They enjoy being loved, appreciated, and supported for being their authentic selves. And they are similarly able to love, appreciate, and support a loving partner. As a result, they enjoy mutually supportive relationships, sensing that they are both lovable and loved.

Preoccupied Attachment

People with this insecure style of attachment feel ill-equipped to cope well with being distressed. They sense that there is something fundamentally flawed about them, such as being inadequate, unlovable, or deficient. Although they believe that other people can be emotionally available and help calm them, they fear not being accepted and loved, because they feel unworthy. So, they often become *preoccupied* with earning acceptance, such as by being especially kind and helpful, earning lots of money, or attaining status. Unfortunately, even when they do feel loved, they tend to perceive that it is the result of their performance or that the other person does not know the real them, not because they are truly cared about for their authentic selves. As a result, they remain forever trying to earn love and prevent rejection or abandonment.

Dismissing Attachment

Those with a dismissing style of attachment cope with difficulties by relying on themselves alone. They view others as not emotionally available to them. Because they expect to be let down or hurt, they tend to remain avoidant (emotionally distant) in relationships, sometimes even denigrating their partners to keep themselves at a safe distance. They essentially dismiss the emotional importance of others to them as well as dismiss or avoid their own distressed emotions. Instead, they tend to pride themselves on being highly self-sufficient, as they focus their energy on navigating the external world.

Fearful Avoidant Attachment

Those with this anxious *and* avoidant style of attachment are in a terrible bind, especially when they feel distressed. They cannot reliably turn inward because they feel deeply inadequate and incapable of soothing themselves. They also cannot comfortably turn to others for help because they experience others as unavailable, rejecting, or hostile. So, while they may try to comfort themselves or get comfort from others, these efforts often fail, leaving them and their relationships in emotional turmoil. They have no clear way of regaining a sense of emotional balance or well-being.

Preparing to Assess Your Attachment Style

By rating your models of self and others, you can determine the attachment style you generally have. You will see a theme of this style in your life. Still, your attachment style can be different across relationships and over time. You might be more or less anxious in your relationships depending on whether you are with romantic partners, family, friends, or coworkers. Research shows that having a securely attached partner can help insecurely attached people become more secure. Your style can change with other experiences, too, and so you will hopefully become less anxiously attached, and more secure, as you complete exercises in this workbook.

Given that a high rating on the model of self is associated with anxious attachment and a high rating on the model of others is associated with avoidant attachment, you can use them to rate your attachment-related anxiety and avoidance.

Rating Your Models of Self and Others

Read the next two paragraphs and use the directions that follow to then fill in the blanks and assess how much you identify with attachment-related anxiety and avoidance in important relationships in your life. The ideas for this exercise come from empirically based questionnaires (Ainsworth et al. 1978; Simpson, Rholes, and Phillips 1996; Collins 1996; Feeney, Noller, and Hanrahan 1994; Griffin and Bartholomew 1994; Brennan, Clark, and Shaver 1998).

Model of Self: Attachment-Related Anxiety

Being totally emotionally close with _____ means everything to me. But _____ doesn't want to be as close as I would like to be, and my desire to be so close often scares them away. In this relationship, I question myself and am concerned that I'm not as good as them. I'm always worried that they don't care about me as much as I care about them. And I also worry all the time about whether they really love me, will stop loving me, or will decide to leave me. (In platonic friendships and intimate relationships, I'm especially worried that they'll find someone else when we are not together.)

Model of Others: Attachment-Related Avoidance

I am an independent, self-sufficient person, so I don't need to be in a close relationship. I prefer not to depend on _____ or to share deeply personal thoughts and feelings. It makes me uncomfortable when _____ wants to depend on me or talk a lot about their thoughts and feelings. When I have problems, I tend to keep them to myself and figure them out on my own, and I'd prefer it if _____ would do the same.

Now, for each of the relationships in the following table, rate your attachment-related anxiety and attachment-related avoidance on a scale of 0 to 10, with 0 being not at all and 10 being that you completely relate. Then place that rating in the table.

	Anxiety Rating 0–10	Avoidance Rating 0–10
General rating across all relationships		
Current romantic partner		
Previous romantic partner:		
Mother (today)		
Mother (during your childhood)		
Father (today)		
Father (during your childhood)		
Other caregiving family member		
Friend:		
Other:		

Using the ratings in this table, you can now determine your specific attachment style.

Discovering Your Attachment Style

Do you have a preoccupied, dismissing, or fearful avoidant style? Is your insecurity deeply entrenched, or do you lean toward having a somewhat secure style? Has your style changed over time or when you have been with different people? Is it different in different areas of your life?

Fill in the graph in figure 2 using your anxiety and avoidance ratings from the preceding table. Use colored markers or pencils, and add a different color line or dot next to each relationship type in the table (for example, red next to general rating, purple next to current romantic partner). Then use the same color when you graph that relationship.

Do the following for each relationship: Find your Anxiety Rating number along the bottom of the graph. Find your Avoidance Rating number along the left side of the graph. Using the appropriate color, place a dot where the two lines intersect. For example, in figure 1, Cindy has an anxiety rating of 6 and an avoidance rating of 2. Jack has an anxiety rating of 9 and an avoidance rating of 4. You may also find it helpful to look at the instructions on my video, "Plotting Your Attachment Style," at https://drbecker-phelps.com/insecure-in-love-workbook or at http://www.newharbinger.com/52175.

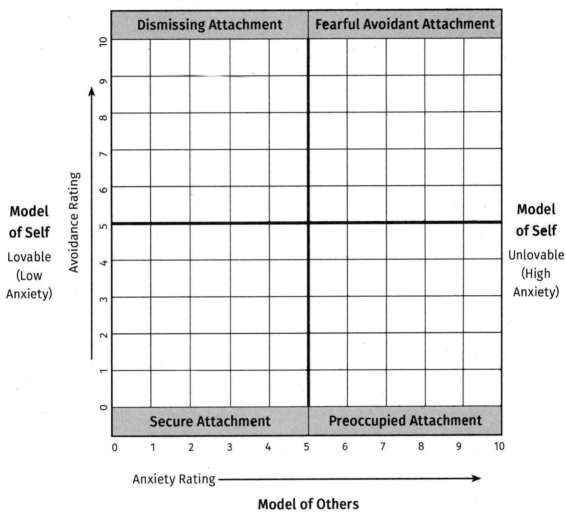

Figure 2

Make note of where each relationship falls, including the quadrant it is in and where it is in that quadrant. Do you see any patterns? For instance, is your style in a particular relationship different now than it was years ago? Is your attachment style different in different kinds of relationships (such as friendships versus romantic relationships)? What other insights do you gain as you look at the graph?

_____

_____

_____

_____

_____

_____

_____

While it can be an enlightening process to use the previous exercises to determine your attachment style (which I strongly encourage you to do), you can also use the self-scoring version of the "Experiences in Close Relationships Revised" survey at www.yourpersonality.net to learn about your attachment style.

Earn Security and Happy Relationships

Now that you have a better understanding of your attachment style, you may be wondering, _Is it possible to develop a more secure attachment style and finally find a happy, intimate relationship? To feel truly at home with a partner?_ The answer is yes, you absolutely can change your attachment style! Research has shown that you can develop more secure attachment—or _earned security_—by learning to nurture a sense of yourself as worthy and lovable, and a sense of others as emotionally available to you. These two factors work together. When you feel worthy enough to take in genuine love from others, this love can help you feel all the more worthy and lovable, and can enable you to consistently return that loving support, which nurtures a continued sense of caring in others toward you. It's a positive feedback loop that is self-perpetuating.

The rest of this workbook will be teaching you to do this: to more fully give and receive love. However, while the explanation of "earned security" paints a pretty picture, it is short on details. To begin with, it says little about how your attachment system works. What are its moving parts? And how can you use this knowledge to help you feel happier in relationships? This is the focus of the next chapter.

CHAPTER 2

Understanding Your Attachment System

When you feel threatened or distressed, your attachment system will kick in, prompting you to direct your attention to attachment figures. As infants, your attachment figures were most likely your caretakers, such as your parents. But as you mature, attachment figures can be anyone, such as teachers, mentors, friends, or anyone else you might expect would be supportive. In a committed romantic relationship, it's especially important to relate to your partner as a healthy attachment figure in your life.

Your partner (and any attachment figure) would ideally offer three basic functions. As you read about each of these functions, consider whether this is actually happening:

Safe haven: When you are upset, you turn to your partner for comfort, support, and even protection.

Secure base: Your partner supports and encourages you to explore your interests, goals, and values in the world. They show a genuine desire for you to continue to grow.

Proximity: You experience your partner as close by emotionally, even when you are physically distant. (Thus the expression "Home is where the heart is.")

It is essential to understand that relationships with attachment figures are not just about what those figures can do for you. Healthy adult relationships involve you and your partner both feeling a sense of proximity as you function as a safe haven and secure base for each other. So, consider your current relationship and ask yourself, *To what extent are we a safe haven and secure base for each other? Do we offer a sense of proximity for each other? How does what I notice help or harm the strength of my relationship?* Use the space provided to reflect.

_____

_____

_____

_____

_____

_____

_____

Also, *collaborative communication* is central to relationships with attachment figures. This means functioning as a team as you work together to communicate, including correcting any miscommunications and talking through tensions. While doing this, each of you is having a powerful effect on how the other person is feeling. Ideally, you are *co-regulating* your emotions, or helping to calm each other's distress and enhance each other's positive feelings. So, learning to develop collaborative communication and to co-regulate your emotions is essential in healthy relationships. You will see evidence of this in the exercises in this chapter, and there will also be more about these skills in later chapters.

What do you think your relationship would be like if you were both strong in offering the three basic functions of attachment and in co-regulating?

_____

_____

_____

_____

_____

_____

_____

_____

No doubt what you've described is a healthier relationship than the one you currently have. To help you work toward this, for now, let's focus on the three basic functions of attachment figures. By strengthening these, you will create a stronger foundation for a healthy relationship in which you and your partner feel cared about and supported.

Safe Haven

Not everyone has someone who is a safe haven in their lives. If you don't turn to anyone for comfort when you are upset, then identifying a potential safe haven in a current relationship or developing a new relationship for this is an essential first step. If you do have a safe haven relationship, you can nurture this element by better understanding its function in your life. Engage in these exercises to help you either create or strengthen a safe haven.

Do You Try to Earn Acceptance and Love?

If you are anxiously attached, you don't have a true safe haven, someone who you perceive will value and support your authentic self. You probably sense that there are things you need to do to "earn" approval.

Write about some ways that you try to earn love. You might find it helpful to answer the following: Do you believe that others will accept or love you only if you are sexually desirable, have achieved success in your career, or are especially nice and caring? Do your attempts to earn love leave you feeling alone and empty? Also, do they prevent you from fully sharing your true self? Even if you are successful in one or more of these areas, this way of thinking can have its downside. For instance, when you achieve some success, do you still fear being rejected or abandoned if you misstep or your partner gets to know the "real you"?

_____

_____

_____

_____

_____

_____

_____

_____

Do you have more to say? If so, continue writing in your journal.

Do You Protest Abandonment?

When children feel upset, their attachment system engages and directs them to seek out a caregiver to comfort them—to seek out a safe haven. If their caregiver is not physically and emotionally available, they become distressed and *protest* against the separation (a term used by the father of attachment theory, John Bowlby). This might include looking for their parent, crying, or having a tantrum. When caregivers physically return or become emotionally available again, they can calm their children, but it becomes more difficult to do when the experiences of separation are more frequent or traumatic.

If this dynamic was commonplace in your childhood, you might be easily triggered into feeling alone or abandoned by your partner and protesting against them abandoning you. Reflect on the following ways that people often protest. Check off the ones you experience or enact in your relationship with your partner, and provide an example. (You will be using these examples in later chapters, as you explore your protests more deeply.)

☐   Frequently seeking emotional reassurance

_____

_____

☐ Frequently seeking help with tasks as a way to stay close

_____

_____

☐ Frequently reestablishing communication (such as reaching out by text or phone or looking for ways to "accidentally" run into your partner)

_____

_____

☐ Needing a lot of physical reassurance (hugs, kisses, sex)

_____

_____

☐ "Playing games" to try reengaging your partner (pretending to have an admirer)

_____

_____

☐ Responding angrily, hoping that your partner will try to appease you and reconnect

_____

_____

☐ Being highly people-pleasing. Also called the _please-and-appease_ or _fawning_ reaction. This refers to overlooking your wants and needs to meet the wants, needs, and wishes of your partner. (This dynamic underlies many codependent relationships.)

_____

_____

☐ Falling into despair, giving up and losing hope that you can connect with your partner. (Here you are no longer protesting.)

_____

_____

What is your reaction to seeing and labeling these dynamics? Record any insights about how they may have developed from your childhood experiences.

_____

_____

_____

_____

_____

_____

_____

_____

Identify Safe Havens in Your Life

List all the people you think of as significant or close in your life:

_____   _____   _____   _____

_____   _____   _____   _____

To determine whether any are safe havens, consider these traits of people who serve as a safe haven:

- Communicates that they really hear and understand you

- Expresses a desire to be there for you when you struggle

- Responds to your distress with caring, reassurance, and support

- Effectively communicates their support and caring

- Provides a comforting presence

Of the people you listed, circle the names of those who embody these characteristics.

Now reflect on these relationships. Is your partner on this list, and are they circled? What does this say about your partner and your relationship? What do you think about the other relationships on the list? Are there ways you can work on turning for support to those you have not circled? Are there certain people you turn to for certain things?

_____

_____

_____

_____

_____

_____

_____

_____

Preparing to Take In Comfort

If you have trouble trusting someone will be there for you even when that person has been reliably supportive when you are upset, you may need to practice allowing yourself to be comforted. This involves helping your body and mind relax.

Make some notes about one situation in which you were upset and felt comforted by someone. If you can think of several examples, focus on the one that you can remember most vividly.

_____

_____

_____

Write about any feelings of comfort, support, and relief that you felt.

_____

_____

_____

_____

Note any anxiety or fears of rejection or abandonment that you may have had.

_____

_____

_____

_____

Hold your hands up in front of you with your palms up. Look at one hand and imagine the feeling of comfort in it (really feel it!). Then look at your other hand and imagine the feeling of anxiety or fear in it (again, feel the experience). To the best that you can, bring your attention to both hands, feeling both experiences at the same time. Finally, bring your attention back to the hand that is holding the feelings of being comforted. Allow yourself to feel soothed and cared about. Choose to let go of the anxiety, which is not needed now because you were, in fact, comforted.

You might repeat this exercise with other situations in which someone has comforted you and you felt it or struggled to feel it. When you are ready, try it with a current situation that you have not reached out to anyone about, especially one involving your partner if they made it to your safe haven list in the previous exercise. Now imagine what it would be like to share your distress. Use the next exercise to help you take the next step.

Seeking Comfort from Your Safe Haven

Practice seeking comfort in relationships that you identify as a safe haven. By learning to do this more often, you will move toward feeling greater relationship security.

Name someone who is a safe haven for you. If your partner is clearly a safe haven for you, try talking with them in this exercise. If you don't have a partner or don't feel safe with them, turn to someone else whom you have identified as a safe haven. Be sure not to self-sabotage by picking someone you'd like to be a safe haven but who has not been comforting or emotionally supportive.

_____

Choose a distressing topic to discuss with this person. Be sure to pick a topic that is uncomfortable to discuss, but that you feel safe enough to address with this person.

_____

_____

_____

Prepare for your conversation. Decide on a good time to talk, which might include making plans for when you can do this. If you think the person might respond with problem solving when you really just want them to listen, be sure to tell them what you want up front. Also, to help alleviate any anxiety you might have about starting the conversation, make some notes here about how you can bring up the topic.

_____

_____

_____

Now you are ready to talk with them. While having the conversation, pay attention to how they are responding. Do they seem to want to be there for you? To want to help you? If you see signs of them caring (even if this is not expressed exactly as you would want), then be sure to pay attention:

- Let yourself take in this caring.

- Attend to any easing of tension or distress.

- Attend to any feelings of warmth.

- Linger on these positive reactions.

- If it feels right, ask for a hug. Physical affection can be very soothing.

This is an exercise that you can repeat with either the same person or different people. It can help you to strengthen your ability to feel truly accepted and comforted while being the real you.

If the exercise did not go as well as you would have liked, reflect on what the problem might have been. For example, you might have started with a topic that left you feeling too vulnerable, or you might have chosen the wrong person to open up to. Make some notes about what you think might have gone wrong and what you can do differently next time.

_____

_____

_____

_____

_____

Try the exercise again, adjusting how you approach it. Or move on from the exercise for now, perhaps returning to it later.

Secure Base

When you can turn to someone as a safe haven, you will hopefully also be able to use your relationship with them as a secure base to support and encourage you to explore yourself separately from that relationship. However, keep in mind that some people who are safe havens do not make good secure bases. So, be sure to adjust your expectations. Still, when you do have secure bases in your life, they can help you develop a sense of independence and autonomy.

Identify Secure Bases in Your Life

While you certainly want a partner who acts as a secure base, it is important to have other relationships where you feel supported and encouraged for being your authentic self. To identify secure bases in your life, begin by copying down the list of people you identified as a safe haven in the exercise "Identify Safe Havens in Your Life."

_____ _____ _____ _____

_____ _____ _____ _____

Circle the name of each person who can be described by this list of traits:

- Shows an interest in what's important to you

- Wants you to be the best version of yourself

- Encourages you to explore your interests

- Is consistent in their support and encouragement

- Is supportive even when you differ in opinion or interests

Place a star next to the circled names of people whom you actually reach out to for support and encouragement in exploring and expressing your true interests. These people function as secure bases in your life. The other people whose names you circled are potential secure bases, should you decide to turn to them for that purpose.

Now that you know the secure bases, and potential secure bases, in your life, you can work on strengthening them. The next exercise provides some guidance for doing this.

Strengthening Your Secure Bases

You can strengthen your actual and potential secure bases to help you feel more secure as you explore yourself and your interests. With multiple secure bases (which hopefully includes a romantic relationship), you can continue feeling supported even when one of your relationships is temporarily strained, someone is not available at the moment, or you have a falling out with someone. This is especially helpful when a romantic relationship ends or you struggle with feeling rejected or betrayed by your significant other.

Strengthening your secure bases involves challenging your fears of rejection or your tendency to be self-reliant by testing the trustworthiness of other people. While you could dive in by talking with them about a subject that is close to your heart and scary to address, it's probably a better plan to start with topics that leave you less vulnerable. Then you can take greater risks over time.

Identify an area of personal importance or growth that you would like to address. Write about interests that you are already exploring, or would like to explore, such as learning to paint, looking to advance your career, or exploring your spirituality.

_____

Choose a supportive person whom you would like to talk with about this topic. You might pick a current or potential secure base (both of which you have identified in the last exercise).

_____

Talk with them about the chosen topic. Be sure that you have sufficient uninterrupted time. Consciously choose to be open to their attempts to support and encourage you. By attending to how you benefit from such interactions, you can strengthen your sense of having a secure base and increase your likelihood to turn to others for this. So, after your conversation, return here to write about your experience. You might also want to write more in your journal.

_____

_____

_____

_____

_____

How Well Do You Balance Autonomy and Closeness?

Ideally, in intimate relationships, you maintain a dynamic balance between feeling encouraged to stay emotionally close for comfort (safe haven) and feeling encouraged to explore your own interests (secure base). With this in mind, the secure style of relationship represented in the pictures below depicts a healthy relationship.

Looking at these circles (representing the "space" overlap between you and the other person), which style do you think best reflects your current relationship or your most recent one?

_____

Anxious Style

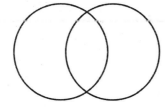

Secure Style

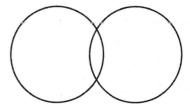

Avoidant Style

The following statements show what partners in these different styles of relationship tend to think. Check off the statements that you identify with wanting in your current or most recent relationship. Note that based on your partner's influence, your personal attachment style might differ from the relationship style you have identified.

Secure Style

☐ *I am comfortable sharing intimate thoughts and feelings with my partner.*

☐ *I enjoy pursuing interests apart from my partner.*

☐ *I feel loved by my partner even when we pursue interests independently.*

☐ *Even when we disagree, I expect that my partner will respect and value my opinions and me.*

☐ *I am comfortable depending on my partner and having my partner depend on me.*

Anxious Style

☐ *I am most comfortable when my partner and I share all of our thoughts, feelings, and interests— when we seem to have merged into one.*

☐ *I am inclined to pursue what my partner enjoys, putting aside my own interests.*

☐ *I am inclined to defer to my partner's values and opinions.*

☐ *Whenever I sense my partner being distant, I feel driven to reconnect (for example, frequently calling or texting), or I act angrily, such as by withdrawing or being nasty.*

Avoidant Style

☐ *I am uncomfortable sharing intimate thoughts and feelings with my partner.*

☐ *I take pride in being self-reliant enough not to need my partner.*

☐ *I am uncomfortable depending on my partner.*

☐ *I am uncomfortable with my partner depending on me.*

☐ *I enjoy pursuing interests apart from my partner.*

Now consider: How well does your relationship meet your needs for a safe haven? During stressful times, how much can you depend on your partner to provide you with a sense of comfort, protection, and support?

_____

_____

_____

_____

How well does your relationship meet your needs for a secure base? How much does your partner support your pursuit of interests and goals apart from your relationship? How well does your relationship support you in feeling good about your sense of who you truly are?

_____

_____

_____

_____

Use your journal to explore and record more thoughts about this, including how well you meet your partner's needs for a safe haven and secure base.

Proximity

Proximity refers to your sense of how close your attachment figure is to you. As an infant, this means physical closeness. As you mature, you develop *mental representations*, which are a sense that your attachment figures exist within you.

Having a mental representation of a consistently available, comforting, and supportive secure base (which involves them being a safe haven, as well) enables you to turn internally to others for emotional support. It also enables you to feel more positively about yourself. As a result, it helps you to have a more secure style of attachment.

Prime Your Secure Base

Research has supported the idea that you can "prime" your secure base by consciously and repeatedly accessing the comfort and encouragement of mental representations (Mikulincer, Shaver, and Pereg 2003). One way to do this is with your mobile phone.

Choose a secure base. Pick someone you have identified in the exercise "Identify Secure Bases in Your Life" from earlier in this chapter. If you have identified your romantic partner as a secure base, you will likely want to pick them. However, as discussed earlier, it's important to nurture more than one secure base, so you can pick someone else for this exercise. Write your chosen secure base here: _____

Find a picture of this person on your phone. While it can be any picture, you might benefit more from choosing a picture that depicts a positive experience you had together.

Save this picture in an easily accessible place on your phone. You might make it your wallpaper or save it in a Favorites album. The idea is that it should be easy to find.

Set an alarm on your phone to look at this picture every day. While this exercise is based on research showing that secure base priming is helpful, there is no clear evidence for the best way to do it or the best frequency. I suggest that you look at this picture at least once or twice a day.

Every time the alarm goes off, prime your connection as a secure base. Look at the picture and do the following. Pause long enough to revisit a memory of this person being caring, supportive, and encouraging. Then fill in the blank in the following sentences with the name of your person. These sentences reflect the three basic elements of secure attachment: proximity, safe haven, and secure base. Repeat the sentences (aloud, if possible) slowly and with a connection to what you are saying (or thinking):

"_____ genuinely cares about me and just being near them is comforting."

"If I am upset, I can ask _____ for help and they will be there for me, if possible."

"I can rely on _____ to support and encourage me in activities that I want to pursue."

Print out or save these sentences on your phone so that you always have them with you. The more you repeat them with a sense of connection to what you are saying, the more they can help you feel closer to your secure base.

To help you grow and heal enough to finally be in the love relationship that you want—in addition to having safe havens and secure bases—it is essential that you take care of some other fundamental physical and emotional needs, especially during stressful times. These topics will be reviewed in the next chapter.

CHAPTER 3

Preparing to Heal

Despite the booming "self-improvement" industry, your authentic self does not need to be improved or repaired for you to be securely happy in love. After all, you are not a car or smartphone. However, you must heal to gain greater security. Unfortunately, your insecurity can interfere with that healing by remaining focused on perceived or feared threats or on your perceived unworthiness, a danger in itself.

At a fundamental level, your body is responsible for your sense of danger. Whether your fears are based in objective outside threats or internally perceived insecurity, your body will respond defensively. Its reactions can interfere with your conscious attempts to correct your thinking, feel more self-assured, or act more confidently. So you must often calm your body before you can begin to make other changes. This chapter helps you to do just that.

Understanding Your Nervous System

Psychiatrist and neuroscientist Stephen Porges developed *polyvagal theory*, which describes neurophysiological mechanisms of attachment theory (Porges and Dana 2018). That is, it describes how the nervous system (neuro) and the rest of the body (physiology) are tied to the attachment system. To be clear, this is a theory that needs further scrutiny and may yet be amended. But whatever the theory's future, it provides a useful framework for helping people manage their body's response to danger.

The theory focuses largely on the *autonomic nervous system*, which controls the typically involuntary actions of your body, such as your heartbeat and breathing. More specifically, polyvagal theory addresses how the autonomic nervous system is responsible for responding to threats and facilitating a sense of safeness and well-being. The autonomic nervous system consists of two main branches. The *sympathetic nervous system* increases your heart rate and gives you energy. The *parasympathetic nervous system* decreases your heart rate and calms you through two main pathways of the vagus nerve—the ventral vagus and dorsal vagus—which I will explain shortly.

When someone feels threatened, the sympathetic and parasympathetic systems engage in a particular order, creating specific states of experience, as shown from top to bottom in the following diagram.

Three States of the Autonomic Nervous System		
In response to externally objective or imagined threat		
Ventral Vagal State:	**Threat:**	
Safety, safeness, connection, well-being	*Perception:* Manageable threat	
	Response: Equanimity, relative calm, seek connection	
	↓	
Sympathetic State:	**Threat:**	
Mobilizing energy	*Perception:* Danger	
	Response: Fight-or-flight response (move toward or away from threat)	
	↓	
Dorsal Vagal State:	**Threat:**	
Immobilized	*Perception:* Life threat, trapped	
	Response: Freeze response, collapsed, numb, shut down, fainting	

Ventral Vagal State

Your body's first line of defense is to use the peripheral nervous system's ventral vagus pathway, which prompts you to try to connect with others and yourself in a way that generally helps you feel safe, calm, and socially engaged. When this pathway is well toned and strong, it can help you respond to threats in a more thoughtful way. It is also linked to a broader, neurologically based *social engagement system* that, when functioning well, allows for secure attachment. It enables you to feel secure and comfortably at home with those you love. One of my patients describes the ventral vagal state as being "in line with the universe."

If the ventral vagal state is not available to someone or it cannot be maintained, their sympathetic nervous system attempts to manage the threat.

Sympathetic State

The sympathetic nervous system mobilizes you with a *fight-or-flight* response. You know the feeling, even if you don't know the term. Two patients I have worked with have labeled this state as "frenetic" and "spun out." Imagine you have parked your car, just getting into the spot before someone else. You look up to see that person angrily approaching you. Your heart begins beating fast, and you feel the urge to fight or flee. You might feel similarly if you stumble upon romantic texts on your partner's phone. An extension of this is the please-and-appease or fawning reaction, which involves being excessively people-pleasing.

If someone's attempt to manage danger with the sympathetic nervous system fails, the dorsal vagal pathway of the vagus nerve takes over and they collapse into a dorsal vagal state.

Dorsal Vagal State

When you sense that a life-threatening (or psychically overwhelming) danger is inescapable, the dorsal vagal pathway offers the body another defense system by immobilizing you with a *freeze* reaction, like a deer in the headlights. You may simply feel unable to get off the couch, be numb, or disconnect with yourself and the world around you. You may even faint.

Before continuing on, I would like to acknowledge that the exercises in this chapter have been influenced by the work of Deb Dana, who has been a strong force in integrating polyvagal theory into therapy. Also, it may be helpful for you to know that you will likely find these exercises difficult. Do the best you can. Attend to what you learn, and consider returning to these exercises later, after you have completed more of this workbook. Remember, this is all about growth!

Getting to Know Your Sympathetic State

People with an insecure attachment style are often in a sympathetic state, that is, in the grips of a fight-or-flight response. When this happens, it can be extremely difficult, if not impossible, for them to see their tendency to view themselves negatively and expect to be judged. For this reason, it can help to identify signs of sympathetic nervous system reactions during a calmer time. Assuming you are feeling relatively calm now, list at least two examples of when you have been in the grips of the fight-or-flight response.

_____

_____

_____

The next step is to describe four domains of awareness—sensations, thoughts, emotions, and actions—about what happened. Allow yourself to briefly experience one of your examples of when you were in the grips of fight-or-flight. Then reflect on it and use the appropriate lines below to describe each domain of awareness. Do the same with your second example, followed by any other examples you listed. You don't need to specify which experiences of fight-or-flight are associated with which examples. By writing them all out on the same line, you can get a sense of what this state looks like. The purpose is to help you recognize your sympathetic state in the future.

Example: *Sam was really upset when Bill dumped him. Sam was devastated when he did not get a promotion.*

Here's how Sam charted his experiences of fight-or-flight:

Sensations: Pounding heart, pit in stomach, nauseated

Thoughts: Disbelief, angry thoughts, pessimistic and negative thinking

Emotions: Hurt, furious, afraid, devastated

Actions: Crying, yelling, sulking, drinking, watching YouTube videos

Now, it is your turn to complete this chart, reflecting on your own experiences of fight-or-flight:

Sensations: _____

_____

Thoughts: _____

_____

Emotions: _____

_____

Actions: _____

_____

The next couple of exercises will help you get to know your two vagal states. Later in the chapter, you will learn how to use this information about the autonomic nervous system to manage your distress better.

Getting to Know Your Dorsal Vagal State

Think of at least a couple of times when you were so distressed that you became immobilized, or had a freeze reaction. You may have fainted, sunk into your couch, or gone through the day with a sense of numbness and disconnection. These are signs of being in a dorsal vagal state. Describe those experiences here.

_____

_____

_____

After looking at the next example, complete the self-awareness chart for your dorsal vagal experiences.

Example: *Stephanie walked in on her husband cheating. Afterward, she told her mother about it, but her mother blamed her.*

Here is Stephanie's self-awareness chart:

Sensations: Numb, too heavy to move

Thoughts: Blank, confused, thoughts of wanting to hide from the world

Emotions: Dazed, deeply hurt, betrayed, stunned, emotionally numb

Actions: Curling up on the couch all day, crying at times, staring at the walls at times

Now it's your turn:

Sensations: _____

_____

Thoughts: _____

_____

Emotions: _____

_____

Actions: _____

_____

Now, thinking of other dorsal vagal state experiences, add any other descriptions that come to mind for each domain. If completing this exercise upsets you, do something active—like going for a walk or talking with a friend—to counter the distress that connecting with this immobilized state can bring.

Getting to Know Your Ventral Vagal State

The ventral vagal state offers a sense of connection and well-being that can help you feel relatively calm and capable. With a strong ventral vagal experience, you can comfort yourself and remain steadfast in effectively managing your experience of feeling threatened and the threats themselves.

Before you complete the ventral vagal self-awareness chart, check out this example: When Jada was facing problems at work with her boss, she would sometimes find a sense of serenity and even awe while sitting in church and contemplating the situation. Jada also liked playing tennis and was good at it, so it helped her let go of stress.

Sensations: Relaxed body, inner calm, beating heart, positive energy

Thoughts: Appreciating the beauty around me, positive and focused thoughts, seeing myself as capable and confident

Emotions: Serene, grateful, content, excited, motivated, confident

Actions: Sitting calmly, observing the world around me, smiling, playing tennis, engaging positively with my tennis partner

Describe at least a couple of times when you were in the ventral vagal state even as you faced difficulty or felt afraid.

_____

_____

_____

_____

Now complete the self-awareness chart:

Sensations: _____

_____

Thoughts: _____

_____

Emotions: _____

_____

Actions: _____

_____

Take a moment to reflect on how good it feels to be in the ventral vagal state. Exercises later in this chapter will help you to practice choosing activities that encourage reexperiencing it.

Getting to Know Your Experience of Danger

Given your insecure attachment, you know all too well the sense of feeling unsafe even when your current circumstance is "objectively" safe. The more distressed you become as your sympathetic nervous system is activated, the harder it is to think clearly and recognize that you are projecting your fears onto your current situation. You end up getting caught in a fight-or-flight or freeze reaction. Another common way of understanding this is that you are out of your *window of tolerance* (Siegel 2010).

You can avoid this problem by learning to identify your increasing arousal at lower levels of intensity. With this awareness, you can choose to calm yourself before you become overwhelmed and your thinking is impaired. For instance, if you are terrified of rejection, you may incessantly text your partner every time they are out with friends and end up in terrible arguments when they return home. However, if you learn to calm your fear before it becomes overwhelming and outside your window of tolerance, you can manage the issue on your own or wait until your partner returns home and have a constructive conversation about your concerns.

Rating Your Levels of Arousal

A helpful step toward remaining within your window of tolerance when you are faced with a problem is to rate your levels of arousal (from 0 to 10). Here is a sample scale from one of my patients. Let's call her Pamela:

Ventral Vagal

0   Nonverbal, peaceful, stillness, feel okay, totally calm, deep and calm breathing

1   Say and feel it is okay, basically calm, relaxed, but need reassurance

2   Feeling okay but not embracing it, responsive, slightly tense, unsure

3   Okay but with doubt, mostly calm, hint of anxiety, getting things done

Sympathetic

4   *Should* be okay, but feeling some anxiety, looking for external cause, uncomfortable (something brewing)

5   *Maybe* something is wrong, not feeling okay, increasing tension, anxious, scared, beginning to snap

6   **Something is wrong**, not okay, thoughts beginning to race, tense, overwhelmed

7   *Not good,* swirling thoughts and feelings, repetitive thoughts, faster breathing

Dorsal Vagal

8   *Everything is wrong,* not good, distressed, very anxious, agitated, frantic breathing, helpless, fatigued

9   Logjam of thoughts of all wrong (*Everything is wrong, I'm wrong*), shut down, crying, hopeless

10   Nonverbal paralyzed, overwhelmed, numb

As Pamela developed this scale, she came to know her overall autonomic nervous system much better. You may notice that she not only created a rating scale of her arousal but also indicated when she saw a shift in her autonomic state experiences.

Reflect on various problems that you have recently had and how you responded. Complete this scale as Pamela did, rating your levels of arousal from 0 to 10, where 0 is the lowest arousal and 10 the highest. You may find it helpful to review your responses in the "Getting to Know" exercises in the previous section. Fill in a description for as many of the rating levels as you can; it's okay if you need to leave some blank. You may be able to fill in the blanks later, after completing more of this workbook. To the left of the table, indicate which numbered ratings belong to each of the three autonomic states.

Review this scale and circle the number or range of arousal that coincides with you not being able to think clearly, as Pamela did by circling 6 and 7. For you, this might involve being confused, unable to understand your own experience, or failing to consider different aspects of the situation beyond your tunnel-vision reactions. Your goal in the future will be to calm your rising arousal before you hit that level.

If you realize that you go from 0 to 10 in a flash, you can help yourself by working on the exercises in the next section. Learning to calm your nervous system and feel safer will give you a chance to slow the rate of your rising arousal. You may be able to describe more and more identifiable levels of arousal before you experience being unable think clearly. Then you will have more opportunity to keep yourself within your window of tolerance and address issues from a calm, safe, ventral vagal state.

Each day, practice rating your level of arousal and naming the autonomic state you are in. This way you can choose to calm your distress before you are overwhelmed by it. The next sections offer ways for you to soothe your nervous system by identifying helpful tools or resources.

How to Soothe Your Nervous System

With an insecure attachment style, you are grounded in your threat system, meaning that you are most often operating from, or are easily triggered into, a hyperaroused reaction of fight-or-flight or a hypoaroused reaction of freeze.

One way to find comfort and support is to identify people who act as safe havens and secure bases in your life, as discussed in chapter 2. The next exercises will help you develop your inner resources and be more open to help from others. They strengthen your model of self as capable and worthy and strengthen your model of others as emotionally available (the building blocks of secure attachment).

List Go-To Activities to Calm Your Distress

When you are in a threat state, you will likely be at a loss for how to comfort yourself effectively, falling back to unhealthy coping, such as emotional eating, isolating, drinking, getting high, or binge shopping. It is often too hard to think of healthier ways to cope at these times, so use this exercise to develop a list of constructive ways to cope that you can have ready when you need it.

Given that secure attachment involves being able to rely on yourself and others when you are distressed, use the table below to list activities you and others can do to help calm and comfort you. Keeping in mind that it is helpful to have a range of options in both lists, use the suggestions below the table to help get you started. Feel free to include options that you don't do, but you are willing to try and think would help.

Ways to Calm Yourself	Ways Others Can Help Calm You

Listening to music	Taking a hot bath	Exercising (specify)
Meditating	Playing an instrument	Reading
Doing yoga	Going to movies	Talking with a friend
Watching a TV show	Playing video games	Spending time in nature
Physical affection	Dancing	Getting a massage
Eating alone or with friends	Doing a craft	Doing something that makes you laugh (specify)

Take a picture of this list on your phone or copy it onto an index card so that you can have ready access to it. Add to the list when you find new activities that help to calm you.

Keep in mind that any of these activities can be overdone. So, if certain ones become problematic, reduce how often you use them, and try another option.

Using Your Breath to Relax

One way that people naturally calm themselves and strengthen their vagal tone is through breathing. Try each of these types of breathing, maybe choosing one to practice on a daily basis:

Mindful breathing: This is very simply attending to your breath. Observe the sensations of inhaling and of exhaling. You might note the sense of air moving through your nostrils, the movement of your belly going up and down, and even the pause at the end of each breath in and out. When you become distracted, gently redirect your attention back to your breath. (The healthiest rate of breathing for our bodies is inhaling for 5.5 seconds and exhaling for 5.5 seconds. It is associated with greater relaxation than other patterns of breathing.)

Deep or diaphragmatic breathing: Imagine that your belly is a balloon. Breathe in through your nose, filling the balloon. Next, exhale slowly through your mouth, deflating the balloon. Take at least five to ten breaths. If you place one hand on your belly and your other hand on your chest, you will notice that your lungs move very little. If you find this difficult, practice by lying on your back with your knees bent.

Square breathing: If you have racing thoughts, the square breathing technique might be especially helpful to do while deep breathing. Inhale deeply to the count of 4. Pause to the count of 4. Exhale to the count of 4. And finally hold to the count of 4. You might also imagine drawing each side of the square in your mind's eye as you count.

Sighing: Deb Dana (2018) strongly advocates sighing as a way to relieve stress. You can enhance this natural response by exhaling as if blowing slowly through a straw.

If you are interested in learning more about breathing, a great resource is the book *Breath: The New Science of a Lost Art* by James Nestor (2020).

Taking Care of the Basics

By maintaining a healthy lifestyle, you can keep yourself feeling stronger, more likely to be in a ventral vagal state, and better able to meet life's challenges. With this in mind, check off each item that needs improving:

☐ Safe living situation

☐ Managing finances

☐ Caring for self when sick

☐ Sufficient sleep

☐ Healthy eating

☐ Regular exercise

☐ Maintaining routine

☐ Strong social connections

☐ Meaningful activities

☐ Enjoyable activities

☐ Connection to something larger (e.g., nature, community)

What about the areas that you checked off make you think that they need improving? What can you do to work on becoming healthier in those areas?

_____

_____

_____

_____

_____

_____

Depending on your struggles in taking care of the basics, you may wish to explore these areas more in depth in your journal.

Introducing STEAM

While the exercises covered in this section can help increase your ventral vagal energy, you will need to shift your inner home from a fear-based state to a safety-based state to become more securely attached. Central to this effort is increasing self-awareness, beyond what you have done with previous exercises. As you gain greater awareness and understanding of yourself, you can develop greater empathy and compassion. This *compassionate self-awareness* will enable you to nurture security within yourself and your relationships.

While the meaning of self-awareness seems apparent, it is a vague term. To clarify it, consider these five basic domains, which I refer to as STEAM: sensations, thoughts, emotions, actions, and mentalizing. You've already done some work with the first four of these, but there is much more to explore. By developing awareness in these five domains, you will expand your connection to each aspect of your experiences.

Developing Self-Awareness by Gaining STEAM

Practice expanding your awareness with STEAM by trying this: Describe a situation with your current or a previous partner (or potential partner) in which you felt anxious or insecure, *but that you also have some understanding and self-compassion for.*

_____

_____

_____

As you recall and relive this situation, enrich your experience by considering each domain of STEAM, and write about it in the space provided.

Sensations. Your emotional experiences are based in your body, so you can feel them on a physical level. Slowly scan your body from your toes to the top of your head. Ask yourself, *What do I sense in my body?* Note any sensations, such as tension in your chest, butterflies in your stomach, or agitated energy rushing through your body.

_____

_____

_____

_____

Thoughts. People have all kinds of thoughts all the time, often without reflecting on them or even realizing it. Ask yourself: *What am I thinking? What do I think about what I'm thinking?*

_____

_____

_____

_____

Emotions. Pay attention to your emotions. You may realize that you have more emotions than you were originally aware of. Sometimes they conflict with each other. Ask yourself, *What am I feeling? What do I feel about what I'm feeling?*

_____

_____

_____

_____

Actions: Make note of simple movements as well as interactions with others, such as fidgeting, smiling, texting, or yelling at someone. Also include urges to act, even if you don't follow through with them. Ask yourself, *What are my actions? What are my reactions?*

_____

_____

_____

_____

Mentalizing. This is basically understanding and connecting with what motivates someone's behaviors, whether it's your behaviors or someone else's. Mentalizing enables you to have self-compassion as well as empathy and compassion for other people. Use awareness from the first four domains to mentalize yourself and others. To mentalize yourself, ask yourself, *What inner experiences are motivating my actions?*

_____

_____

_____

_____

_____

To mentalize the other person, make an effort to see the world through their eyes. Ask yourself, *What do I think the other person's inner experiences are that motivate their actions?*

_____

_____

_____

_____

Reflect on how exploring STEAM has affected your experience of this situation. Has it increased your empathy and compassion for yourself? Has it helped you to have a greater appreciation of the other person's experience? Has it prompted any insights? Did you have great difficulty with any particular part of it?

_____

_____

_____

_____

_____

This exercise was designed to be within your ability to respond positively to yourself and perhaps the other person. With repetition, you will strengthen your compassionate self-awareness and compassionate other-awareness and be able to apply it to more insecurity-inducing circumstances. To practice, use the "Gain Self-Awareness Through STEAM" worksheet to repeat this exercise. You can access it online at https://drbecker-phelps.com/insecure-in-love-workbook or at http://www.newharbinger.com/52175.

The next part of this workbook further explores the five domains of self-awareness in STEAM. By becoming compassionately self-aware in these domains, you will get to know yourself better and welcome home your true self, creating a greater sense of personal well-being and improving your ability to nurture secure relationships.

CHAPTER 4

STEAM: Sensations

Have you noticed your body often feeling unsettled or tense, hyper-attuned to the possibility of your partner (or love interest) judging or leaving you? If you have, this is partly because the human attachment system is based on the body's attunement to danger—or problems—and safety. However, your insecure attachment makes you especially sensitive to actual or potential threats.

Think about the terror anybody might feel when unexpectedly coming face-to-face with a coyote while hiking, as well as the comfort they might feel when hugged by a trusted friend after escaping from that coyote. In addition to such obvious examples of danger and safety, your body can also perceive less obvious examples outside of your conscious awareness and have reactions beyond your direct control (a process called *neuroception*). For instance, years ago, I remember having the eerie sense that someone was watching me in my college bedroom, only to then realize that our cat was perched on top of the door and peering down on me. Have you ever had a bodily reaction to sensing that you were potentially in danger or something "bad" was going to happen?

While your physical sensations occur within the context of having a sense of danger or safety, they also reflect more specific emotions. For example, imagine feeling safe while picnicking on a sunny day with a caring partner. Your skin will be warm from the sun. If you are enjoying a lazy day together, your body might be relaxed and you might feel serenely happy. But, as an anxiously attached person, you might also feel vulnerable and fear judgment even though your partner is lovingly attentive. So, rather than relaxing into the romantic moment, your muscles might tighten with distrust and suspicion.

By learning to tune in to your bodily sensations, as you will do in this chapter, you can become fully and consciously attentive (or *mindful*) of them, more aware of the emotions that accompany them, and more aware of how they affect your perceptions of yourself and others. Altogether, this awareness can help you to empathize with, and have compassion for, emotional struggles associated with your sensations. It also creates an opportunity for you to choose to act in ways that can calm your body and nurture a sense of safety. As a result, you can foster a greater sense of well-being within yourself and in relationships with others.

Attend to Your Sensations

Getting to know your sensations begins with simply choosing to be mindful. You can pay attention to your body while doing anything, such as brushing your teeth, listening to music, or chopping vegetables. In this exercise, you will pay attention to the sensations that accompany an increasingly large smile.

With your face in a neutral expression, notice the sensations in your face and the rest of your body. Note muscle tension in your forehead, around your eyes, in your cheeks, and along your jaw. Observe other sensations, such as tingling, pain, or a tickle. Also make note of sensations in the rest of your body. Describe your experience:

_____

_____

_____

Next, turn the corners of your mouth up slightly. Describe the sensations you experience:

_____

_____

_____

Now lift your mouth into a full smile, and note what you observe:

_____

_____

_____

Make as broad a smile as your muscles will allow. Describe what you notice:

_____

_____

_____

Reflect on the exercise as a whole and describe any observations or insights. (For instance, I notice an increasing lightness in my chest as I move from a neutral expression to a full smile, but a subtle tightness takes over when I mimic the Joker's overly full satanic grin. I associate the lightness in my slight and full smile with being happy.)

_____

_____

_____

_____

What Your Body Remembers

In chapter 3, you explored the three states of your autonomic nervous system: ventral vagal (safe, connected), sympathetic (fight-or-flight), and dorsal vagal (freeze). You may have noticed that your body tends to be at home in, or easily drift back to, the latter two states. If that's the case, your body has learned to be particularly attuned to the possibility of being harmed. This raises an interesting and important question: what taught your body to remain prepared for danger?

Many people who feel constantly on guard have felt that way since childhood when they felt physically or emotionally unsafe. Similarly, you may have a history of physical, sexual, or emotional abuse or a history of neglect. Or if you don't think your childhood was traumatic, you may still have felt deeply unheard, misunderstood, or alone in taking care of things at too young an age. Any of these experiences is enough to leave a lasting imprint on your body's nervous system, priming it to operate from a sense of danger even when you are objectively in a safe environment.

It's worth noting that the human body can also retain its reactions with less extreme or chronic threats, though they tend to be more situation-specific. This explains why my accidentally eating a bug years ago in a restaurant still induces a wave of nausea when I just pass by that place today. Have you had similar experiences that stick with you?

If your body tends to be on guard for potential danger, understanding the origins of this bias can offer insight into your current tendency to feel angry or fear rejection (fight-or-flight reactions) or to become emotionally numb or despondent (freeze reactions). And this insight can help you to heal, feeling emotionally safer and more secure.

What Do You Remember?

Think about recent experiences of your body being in a fight-or-flight or freeze state, especially when your reactions did not seem to fit with the situations. Ask yourself, *When have I felt like this before?* Be open to all memories, but give particular attention to the earliest ones. Do you see a pattern of feeling emotional in the face of particular physical or emotional threats? Or feeling emotional when there are no obvious threats in the moment? As you think about this, do you understand how your body may have become trained to remain primed for threats? Can you understand how your current reactions may sometimes be more about your body doing what it was trained to do rather than truly responding to the current situation? (There is a lot to consider here, so feel free to continue writing about this in your journal.)

_____

_____

_____

_____

_____

As you complete this exercise, be patient and kind to yourself. People spend years in therapy working to identify such patterns and nurture healthier responses. Consider it an open-ended exercise that you can continue in your journal. Gaining greater awareness and understanding of your body's experiences is an important part of developing compassionate self-awareness and moving toward more secure attachment.

What Your Senses Can Tell You

With a practice of attending to your body, you can improve your ability to recognize physical reactions to emotions, such as noticing your jaw tense with anxiety when your partner flirts with strangers. According to one study, young children have similar bodily experiences for different emotions, but those experiences become more differentiated as children mature into adulthood (Hietanen et al. 2016). Research also suggests that sensations related to emotions weaken as adults age, likely leading us to be less aware of our sensations and to rely more on processing our emotions cognitively (Volynets et al. 2020).

Though your sensations are only one domain of self-awareness, they can help you to connect more fully with your *self* by serving as a portal to awareness in other domains. For instance, you may realize that you are in love when you notice that just thinking about your partner makes your heart pound.

Mapping Your Senses and Emotions

To gain greater awareness of emotion-related sensations, use the following body outlines to map out where you feel emotions. You will need red, yellow, blue, and black pencils, markers, or crayons.

For each figure, first imagine experiencing the emotion associated with it, and then fill in the parts of the figure using these colors to represent aspects of your bodily sensations:

Yellow: Most intense, surging energy

Red: Active energy

Blue: Slow energy

Black: Lack of energy, numbness, or unmoving heaviness

Example: *Ron was furious, which caused his heart to feel like it was beating out of his chest, his hands to clench in fists, his legs to go numb, and his thoughts to race. He completed the body outline exercise by coloring his head and chest yellow. His arms were red with some yellow but became all yellow in his hands. He also colored his legs black.*

After coloring in each figure, use the space underneath it to describe your sensations or physical experiences, such as tightness, heaviness, or a sense of flowing energy.

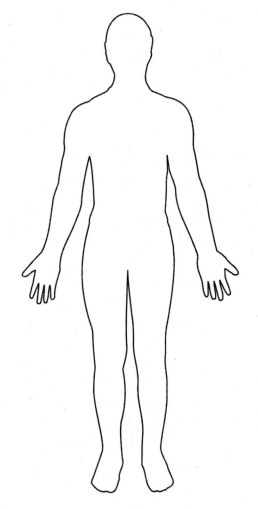

Nonemotional state

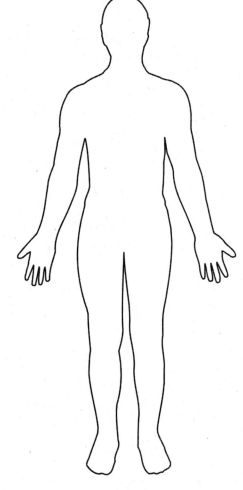

Sadness

_____

_____

_____

_____

_____

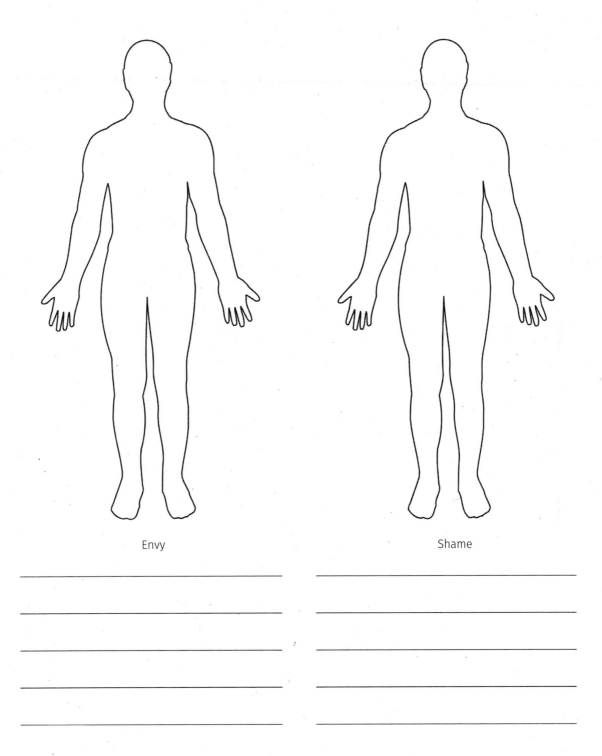

Envy

Shame

_____   _____

_____   _____

_____   _____

_____   _____

_____   _____

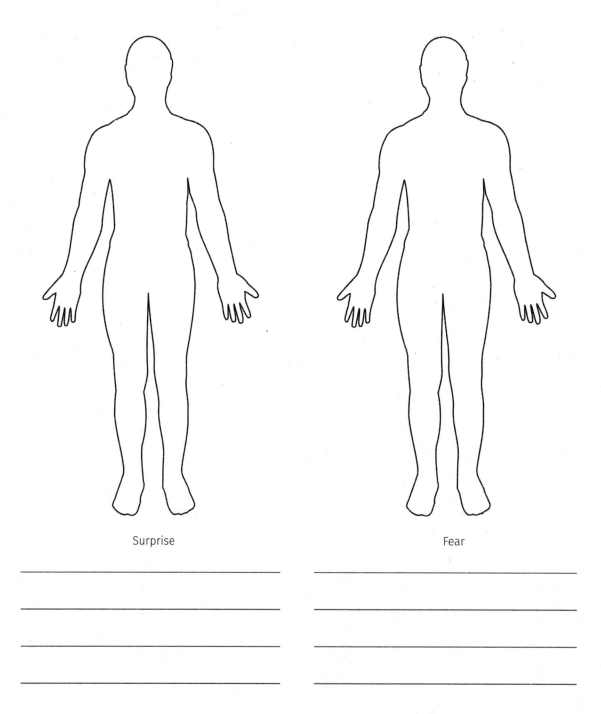

Surprise

Fear

_____   _____

_____   _____

_____   _____

_____   _____

_____   _____

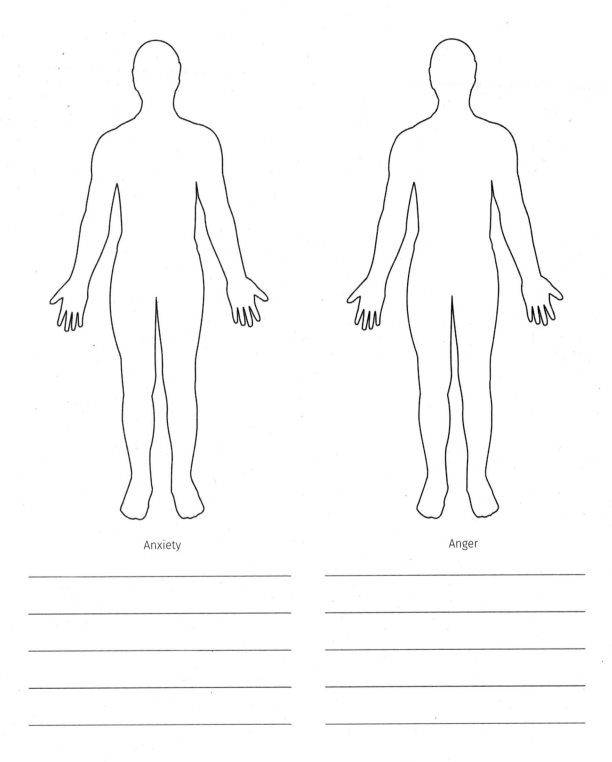

Anxiety

Anger

_____   _____

_____   _____

_____   _____

_____   _____

_____   _____

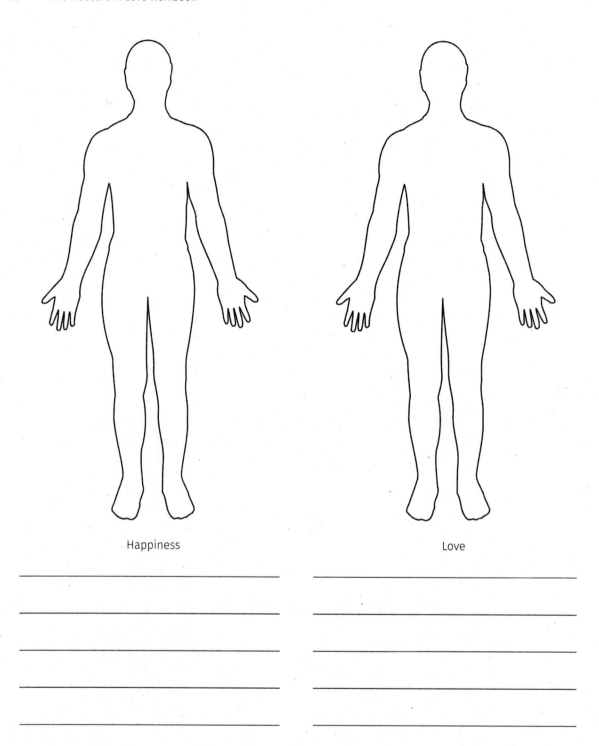

Happiness

Love

_____   _____

_____   _____

_____   _____

_____   _____

_____   _____

Reflect on any insights from this mapping exercise and write about them in your journal. You might want to think about situations in which your reaction did not make sense to you. If you accept that your body was having this reaction for a reason, think about what experiences in your life might have trained your body to react as it did. You may want to review your reactions again after you have gained more personal insight by completing all of the STEAM chapters.

Does Calm Feel Safe or Threatening to You?

When people are overcome by a sense of threat, they move out of their window of tolerance, and their ability to cope is compromised. For instance, if the person you are dating begins ghosting you, your anxious attachment style might go into overdrive, urging you to send long strings of text messages or shout obscenities into their voicemail. While sitting calmly reading this book, you might think that the obvious thing to do is calm down before taking action, and this is certainly a good idea. But it might also backfire.

Your reaction is based in neuroception, the nervous system's assessment of, and reaction to, risk. If you attempt to calm down while perceiving a threat, you are trying to override your nervous system's reaction to danger. It is like telling your body to relax as a dog a few feet ahead begins snarling at you. While you might initially feel calmer, your threat system will become reactivated, causing you to rebound with an intense fight-or-flight or freeze reaction. Does this sound familiar? Unlike securely attached people who can use their calmer state to recognize and manage an overreaction, calming down can leave you feeling vulnerable and pull you back to feeling threatened. Similarly, when you are truly feeling safe and happy, your body might react with feeling vulnerable and migrate back to feeling on alert or immobilized, which you experience as your nervous system's home state. Importantly, these reactions do *not* reflect a fundamental problem with how you think. Rather, your tendency to feel threatened is wired into your nervous system.

By contrast, the bodies of people with secure attachment are primed to operate from a sense of safety and to cope well with stresses, enabling them to be resilient. As you complete the exercises in this workbook, you are training your body to respond in this way, too.

Get to Know Your Body's Responsiveness

When you are relatively calm, practice one of the types of breathing reviewed in the chapter 3 section "Using Your Breath to Relax." Do it for about ten breaths. Observe your body's reaction and describe it:

_____

_____

_____

Now induce a sympathetic fight-or-flight state by reflecting in detail about a moderately upsetting situation. Really take yourself back to that time. What sensations do you notice in your body when you remember the event?

_____

_____

_____

_____

Next, redirect your focus back to breathing again until you feel your body begin to relax. Then continue focusing on your breath a little longer. People sometimes feel more relaxed or more anxious, or notice that they relax briefly and then feel an increase in anxiety. What changes have you noticed in your sensations?

_____

_____

_____

_____

If your body reacts with increased anxiety, reflect on how this is its attempt to keep you safe— even if you consciously know that you are not in immediate danger. Just knowing this can enable you to question your body's message that you are in danger.

Know Your Body's Safety-Threat Balance

Have you noticed that you can be happily in love only to—in the blink of an eye—be miserable for seemingly no good reason? Maybe your partner appears distant one morning, or you think that your happiness must mean that you are blind to some problem. The next thing you know, you are coming undone from anxiety, fear of rejection, or despair.

Because struggles arise in every relationship, it is essential to learn how to acknowledge your concerns without allowing them to override all the good in your relationship. To help you with this, think of a situation in which you have felt distress in your current or a previous relationship, but not enough to totally overwhelm you. For example, maybe you thought your partner was upset with you for leaving your stuff all over again. Briefly describe that situation:

_____

_____

For this exercise, read through all of the directions carefully before following them. The directions are complicated, so you might also want to listen to them on an online recording at https://drbecker-phelps.com/insecure-in-love-workbook or at http://www.newharbinger.com/52175.

Sit comfortably and close your eyes. Hold your hands in front of you, elbows bent, with your palms up. They will act as a scale. As one hand goes up, the other will go down an equal amount, depending on the "weight" of what you sense (as described next). When they are of equal weight, your hands will be level with each other. Take three deep breaths, being sure to slowly and fully exhale. Now imagine your chosen scene in your mind's eye. Then do the following:

In one hand, imagine that you are holding the safe, connected energy you feel in your relationship. Make an effort to really feel the sense of safety. You might notice your facial muscles slacken, your shoulders relax, or your stomach unclench. The more you sense the safety energy, the more you lower that hand, causing your other hand to rise.

Then attend to the other hand. In it, imagine that you are holding the threat-based fight-or-flight sympathetic energy in this situation. You might feel your chest muscles tense, your eyebrows knit together, or the corners of your mouth tug down. Again, the more you connect with the threat energy, the more you lower this hand, causing your other hand to rise.

If you feel the threat energy bringing your hand down lower than your other hand, try refocusing on the positive, safe energy in that other hand. Then see if you can open your awareness so you have a more balanced experience of holding both. You may need to go back and forth several times. You may also want to end the exercise by focusing on the sense of safeness that your loving partner brings you.

If the hand holding your threat-based energy drops like an anchor, practice soothing your nervous system by using the tools you identified in "How to Soothe Your Nervous System" in chapter 3.

Note your observations and reactions related to this exercise:

Attending to Sensations of Inadequacy

When you struggle with feeling unworthy of love, find a quiet place where you can sit undisturbed for at least ten minutes. Do this simple mindfulness practice:

Focus on your body. Be openly aware of your body's sensations, or slowly scan your entire body beginning with your feet. Pause and make note of any pronounced sensations. For example, you might notice churning in your stomach, tension in your chest, or tears in your eyes.

Allow your attention to settle on one of your sensations. Observe it without trying to change it, though it might change on its own. That's okay. Just keep paying attention. If you feel numb, then pay attention to that. As you attend to your sensations, you will become distracted. Each time you do, simply choose to refocus on your body.

Because it can be difficult to remain mindful of sensations, you may want to return to this practice at various times during your journey toward compassionate self-awareness. You might also want to use it as a daily practice, helping you become more conscious of your body and aware of what it is telling you, along with using it as a way to connect with your emotions.

Explore Self-Criticism with Your Sensations

When you are aware of feeling inadequate and self-critical, take a few deep sighs (being sure to fully exhale) and complete this exercise.

Describe the situation that is triggering this reaction:

_____

_____

_____

_____

_____

Imagine that your thoughts are actually a dialogue between two selves: a critic and a victim of that critic. Identify first with the critical self, harshly addressing the victim self as "you." Write down what this voice is saying:

_____

_____

_____

_____

While identifying with the critic, focus on your sensations as you repeat these words aloud or in your head, closing your eyes if it helps. Be sure to say them with feeling. Your sensations will be tightly tied to your emotions, so pay attention to all of the sensations and emotions you experience. Record them in the "Critical Self" column of the following table.

Now, from the perspective of your victim self, review these self-critical comments. What does this victim self say in response?

_____

_____

_____

_____

While continuing to identify with your victim self, repeat these words with feeling, and focus on your sensations and related emotions. Record them in the "Victim Self" column of the table.

Critical Self Sensations and Emotions	Victim Self Sensations and Emotions

Completing this exercise can be very emotional, so you may find it helpful to regain a sense of inner balance by taking a break. Do something to help you clear your head and calm your nervous system.

Once you feel calm, look at the chart and reflect on the relationship between your critical and victim selves. How do your sensations differ depending on which self you identify with? How do these selves affect each other? As a compassionate observer, what are your reactions to this inner struggle? (If you have trouble with this last question, how would a supportive friend respond to you?)

_____

_____

_____

_____

_____

_____

After completing this exercise, you might find it helpful to use your journal to reflect on other specific examples of self-criticism or on how this dynamic between your critical and victim selves affects your life in general. After completing the other STEAM chapters, you may also want to add to what you've written here, or you may want to repeat this exercise.

Open to Sensing Nature

Significant research shows that there are many cognitive, emotional, and physical health benefits of exposure to green spaces (grass, trees, and so on) and blue spaces (water). As researcher Gregory Bratman and his colleagues (2019, 6) explained, the way and the amount that experiences are "absorbed" is essential. For instance, imagine the very different experiences of three people on a beach: one is intently engaged in videos on their phone; one is aware of the distinctive smell of the ocean air while visually taking in the surf and their natural surroundings; and the third person is bodysurfing the waves.

You can enhance your own awareness of nature and the sense of well-being you can derive from it by consciously opening yourself to your senses. Use this mindful walking exercise to guide you: Bring this workbook to someplace in nature. Walk slowly so that you can consciously attend to your sensations—maybe even touch or hold things along the way. If you become distracted, gently redirect your attention to your sensations. More specifically, attend to what you perceive with your senses:

- Sight

- Touch

- Hearing

- Smell

- Taste (You may taste something in your mouth or have a sense of taste from something you smell.)

- Proprioception (This is a sense of posture, balance, position, and movement of your body parts. It enables you to stand up straight and to touch your navel without looking.)

When you complete your mindful walk, return here to record your experiences. Note any insights, such as a greater appreciation of nature or for your body's ability to walk. You might also want to write about how doing this exercise affected your thoughts, emotions, and even what actions you took (or plan to take) afterward.

_____

_____

_____

_____

_____

_____

_____

_____

_____

_____

The exercises in this chapter are just a few ways to open yourself to your sensations. Consider repeating them or doing other activities to enhance your attunement to bodily sensations. Again, sensations weave together with other domains of STEAM to give you a richer sense of yourself. The next chapter will explore the domain of thoughts.

CHAPTER 5

STEAM: Thoughts

Though thoughts fill your mind all the time, you probably rarely notice them, just as you rarely notice the ground beneath your feet. An exception, of course, is when something demands your attention, such as when you trip over a crack in a sidewalk or when distracting thoughts create a problem. For instance, Kathy realized just how caught up she was in fretting about her relationship problems only after her supervisor called her out for not responding to a question.

By learning to attend to your thoughts, you will begin to see patterns in how you think, noticing how you perpetuate certain struggles in yourself and in your relationships. You can also learn more about how your thoughts interact with your sensations, emotions, and actions. With these insights, you can develop a more positive perspective of yourself and be more fully open to support and encouragement from others.

Clarifying Your Emotional Thinking

Have feelings of insecurity sometimes hijacked your thinking? When you experience yourself as flawed or you can't trust others to be there for you (perhaps because of your perceived unworthiness), then you may see the world as affirming what you believe…even when it doesn't.

There are many common patterns of this emotional thinking, often called *faulty* or *dysfunctional* thinking. Review the ones described here. For those that you engage in, write your own example in the space provided. By recognizing these patterns of thinking, you can begin to question them. As you do, you may still believe these thoughts, but they will not feel quite as real to you.

Overgeneralization: After a negative experience, you draw a conclusion that is more general than what the evidence suggests. This type of thinking is marked by absolutes, such as "always," "never," "all," "none," "everyone," and "no one." Example: *After Don's friend made a joke at his expense, he was sure that no one really liked him and he was the butt of everyone's jokes.*

Your example: _____

_____

_____

Mental filter: You tend to see situations as reflecting negatives about you, such as being flawed, unlovable, or worthless. You also tend to minimize or be blind to positives about you. Example: *Although Mark was attentive* *throughout the evening, walked Susan to her car after their first date, and asked if he could call her again, she still thought that she was too boring and he was not interested in her.*

Your example: _____

_____

_____

Personalization: You tend to see yourself as the center of problems. You incorrectly blame yourself or take too much blame for problematic situations. You believe generally stated comments are directed at you. Example: *When Jill's partner became addicted to drugs, Jill blamed herself for not being loving enough or for somehow failing her partner.*

Your example: _____

_____

_____

Shoulds: You expect yourself to (or believe you "should") maintain unrealistically high standards, and you are harsh with yourself for not living up to them. Example: *Every time Bobbie got angry, Blair blamed himself for not saying things the right way.*

Your example: _____

_____

_____

Catastrophizing: You are quick to see situations as worst-case scenarios, whether you are anticipating them, observing them in the moment, or reflecting back on them. Example: *Brad wouldn't outwardly disagree with his girlfriend about anything, because he feared that she would break up with him if he did.*

Your example: _____

_____

_____

To help free yourself from the grips of emotional thinking, pay attention to it during the week. Use your journal to make brief notes about the kind of emotional thinking you get pulled into. As you become more aware of the types of emotional thinking that you engage in, you will be better able to see how it increases your self-criticism, your struggles with feeling inadequate, and your insecurity in your relationships. What once felt like just a reality will begin to seem less true, potentially to the point of your letting go of it.

Identify Common Struggles Within You

To help you identify your insecure thinking, check off each of the following common thoughts and beliefs that you frequently experience. Then place a star next to the two or three statements that occupy your thoughts most often.

☐ *I worry a lot about whether people will like me.*

☐ *I worry a lot about whether people will stop liking me.*

☐ *I worry a lot about people abandoning me.*

☐ *I believe others would not like me if they really knew me.*

☐ *If I disagree with people, they will reject me.*

☐ *I want to be closer to people than they want to be with me.*

☐ *People will only value me if I meet their expectations.*

☐ *I must be perfect or near perfect to value myself or see myself as capable.*

☐ *I am not as good or worthy as other people.*

☐ *I am flawed, deficient, incompetent, and unlovable.*

☐ *Even when others seem to value me, I feel unworthy.*

☐ *If I sometimes look to others for help, it means that I am weak.*

Write down an example for each of the statements that you have starred.

1. _____

   _____

2. _____

   _____

3. _____

   _____

Reflect on the starred statements and your examples. How do these ideas affect your self-image and your relationships? Try to think about them objectively, or imagine what a friend's reaction to them might be. Even though they might feel true, do you objectively think that they are true? Or are they examples of emotional thinking?

_____

_____

_____

_____

_____

_____

_____

_____

_____

_____

_____

You may want to continue exploring your thoughts in your journal. It might help to identify more examples and practice separating what "feels true" from what you more objectively believe is true.

How Self-Verification Maintains Your Insecurity

When it comes to your self-perceptions, you often remain blind to your emotional thinking by unconsciously verifying what you already believe about yourself. As a result, you perpetuate it. According to research by Swann and his colleagues (2003), you can self-verify in three ways. Read about each one, and then write a personal example for it after the example given:

Selective attention: You are especially attuned to observations that confirm or could possibly confirm your sense of being flawed and unlovable. Example: *Ann kept wondering why Chase did not call her Friday night, despite Chase explaining that she had to help her mother then. Ann was sure that Chase could have called if she wanted to, and she stewed about how she was not pretty enough for Chase.*

Your example: _____

_____

_____

Selective memory: You tend to remember feedback that confirms your sense of being unworthy of love. Sometimes you may not even process information that conflicts with your preconception, let alone remember it over time. Example: *Jessica often ruminates about when Ben ended their relationship two years ago. Rather than remembering all the times that he lied and demeaned her, she repeatedly recalls certain incidents that she thinks reveal how she caused the demise of their relationship.*

Your example:_____

_____

_____

Selective interpretation: You tend to interpret potential evidence, the lack of evidence, or ambiguous evidence for you being unlovable as confirmation of that self-perception. If something conflicts with that belief, you explain it away. Example: *Stephen often thinks about how he was dumped by the last three women that he dated. This proves to him that he is a loser even though he was unhappy in two of those relationships. In addition, the fact that there were recently two attractive women who wanted to date him, but he was not interested in, does not lessen his sense that something is wrong with him.*

Your example: _____

_____

_____

Explore How You Self-Verify

By more fully understanding how you verify your sense of being unworthy (to the extent that you feel this way), you can begin to question your self-perceptions. As a result, their hold on you will weaken. With this in mind, describe an interaction in which you felt inadequate or unlovable but your self-perception did not match the situation. For instance, maybe your partner wanted to snuggle up and watch a movie together or a friend phoned you just to chat. Both of these situations clearly cast doubt on your self-perceptions.

_____

_____

_____

To gain greater insight, refer to this situation as you answer the following questions to challenge yourself in these three areas of self-verification.

Challenging selective attention: How did you initially think about the other person's positive responses to you? For instance, did you ignore, dismiss, or minimize them? Did you doubt the honesty or competence of the other person? Or did you focus on negatives while ignoring the more positive feedback?

_____

_____

_____

_____

If you had seen the situation as it truly was, instead of with selective attention, how would that have changed your experience, including how you responded?

_____

_____

_____

_____

Challenging selective memory: In what specific ways did the person show they appreciated you? Be sure to include everything. Nothing is too insignificant. By doing this, you will be more likely to remember their message that you are worthy or lovable.

_____

_____

_____

_____

Challenging selective interpretation: If you did not fully take in the other person's positive responses to you, do you think you could have misinterpreted their motivation or intentions? For example, did you misperceive their tiredness as them not feeling positive toward you? Or did you avoid taking in their positive sentiment by focusing more on previous situations that have upset you?

_____

_____

_____

_____

Review your responses for the three ways that you self-verified your sense of unworthiness in your example. What themes do you see? For instance, you might notice that you were prepared for rejection or that you were critical of yourself. How is reflecting on the ways you self-verify affecting your thinking?

_____

_____

_____

_____

You can review these questions frequently for different situations to gain a greater awareness of the patterns you have already identified and to discover others. You might want to journal to help you think more deeply about what you are noticing. You might also find it helpful to talk about this with a supportive partner or another person you trust.

Social Media and You

When you are on social media, how often does it make you feel connected to others and good about yourself? Or do you tend to judge yourself as inferior and lacking…even when you know that others are projecting an overly positive image? If you fall into the latter category, you are far from alone. People who struggle with their self-image tend not only to compare themselves unfavorably but also to simulate an online identity they think others will like, which only makes them feel worse about themselves.

With some self-analysis and effort, you can join those who use social media to their advantage. This exercise is designed to help you reflect on your use of social media and make conscious choices to do more of what improves your life and less of what hurts it.

Think about the following questions and use the chart below to help organize your thoughts (if you need more space, you can continue the chart in your journal): Which social media platforms do you use? What do you use them for? If you have multiple motivations for one platform, put each one in a separate row (for example, keep up with friends, follow famous people, learn about a topic). How does using this platform affect the way you think about yourself and others? (You might also note what emotions it stirs up in you, or return to do this after completing chapter 6.)

Social Media Platform	Motivation to Use It	Effect on Self and Self-Perceptions	Effect on Perceptions of Others
Example: Facebook	Keep up with friends	I like seeing what they are up to. But then I get sucked in. I compare my accomplishments to others—and I don't measure up. I feel inadequate.	I am impressed by my friends. But sometimes I question their values.

Social Media Platform	Motivation to Use It	Effect on Self and Self-Perceptions	Effect on Perceptions of Others

After completing this chart, reflect on the patterns you see. What do you think you would benefit from doing less of? What might you benefit from doing more of? Example: I can see that I tend to get swept up in looking at my friends on Facebook. What begins as something I'm enjoying ends up with me feeling envious and down on myself. So, I would definitely benefit from being on there less.

_____

_____

_____

_____

_____

At this point, if you want to make a commitment to change your use of social media, state that commitment as clearly and specifically as you can. Example: I am only going to look at Facebook once a day for no more than thirty minutes. If I get caught up in feeling negatively about myself or my friends, I will remind myself of their struggles. If I don't know what struggles they have, I will remind myself that everyone has them. I will also ask myself, "Do I really want to be doing the things they are doing?" (The answer is often no!) If there are specific things I want to add to my life, then I can work on that. I will also write out all the positive things in my life that I can look at when I struggle with this. I will add all of this to a reminder in my Notes on my phone so that I have it whenever I'm looking at Facebook.

_____

_____

_____

_____

_____

_____

_____

_____

Before acting on your plan, be sure to decide whether you are ready to make this change. If you are not ready or are even unsure, just flag what you have written as something you want to return to another time. Also, if you try to do it and are unsuccessful, that's okay. Change is difficult. Rather than become angry with yourself, again flag the exercise as one that you want to return to after you have worked to develop compassionate self-awareness, which can help you to work constructively and effectively toward meeting your goals.

Are You Caught in the Pursuit-Withdrawal Dance?

One of the most common problematic relationship dynamics is the pursuit-withdrawal pattern between anxiously attached and avoidantly attached partners. Although these situations more often involve women who are anxious and men who are avoidant, there are many queer couples with this pattern, as well as heterosexual couples with the opposite pattern. As you read about this dynamic, consider whether you play it out in your life.

Like a passionate dance, the partners are pulled together with a powerful attraction. As the anxious partner steps forward to get the closeness they crave, the avoidant partner steps back to maintain distance (which feels safer). The anxious partner steps in again (protesting abandonment or rejection), prompting the avoidant person to step back. After repeating this dance several times (or more), the avoidant partner may leave. However, this can also go on for years and even continue well into a marriage. Eventually, the anxious partner may despair of ever getting their emotional needs met and finally walk away. Though the avoidant partner, who just wanted to maintain the right distance, might try to reengage them, it may very well be too late.

Reflecting on a current or past relationship, can you see yourself in this dance? If you can, complete the following exercise.

Examine Your Pursuit-Withdrawal Pattern

First, identify which of you is anxiously attached and write their name at the top of the first column. Then write the avoidantly attached person's name at the top of the second column. Next, check off any of the phrases underneath these headings that express your thinking or what you imagine your partner is thinking. If you have trouble "getting inside" your partner's head, you might ask your partner (if appropriate) or talk with a supportive friend who knows them well.

Anxiously Attached Partner	Avoidantly Attached Partner
☐ *I'm not a priority.*	☐ *I just try to do what they want, so they won't get angry.*
☐ *I have to take care of everything.*	☐ *I never do anything right in their eyes.*
☐ *If only I was better (such as smarter, more attractive), they'd be more interested in me.*	☐ *I can never make them happy.*
☐ *We don't do anything together.*	☐ *I don't know what to do to make them happy.*
☐ *They don't care how I feel.*	☐ *They're never interested in sex.*
☐ *They're never around.*	☐ *They're too needy.*
☐ *They never give me anything for my birthday.*	☐ *They're too emotional.*
☐ *They don't care what I think.*	☐ *They have so much baggage.*
☐ *They aren't affectionate at all.*	☐ *They're always upset about something.*
☐ *There's no romance or passion in our relationship.*	☐ *I'd be better off alone.*
☐ *They're going to leave.*	

Write about how the statements that you checked off are part of the pursuit-withdrawal dynamic in your relationship.

_____

_____

_____

_____

_____

_____

_____

Depending on your relationship, you might want to talk with your partner about this. Challenge yourselves to fully understand each other's thoughts and feelings. This can help you work cooperatively to change the pattern.

Now that you have identified and reflected upon your thoughts, we turn our attention to your emotions.

CHAPTER 6

STEAM: Emotions

Who are you, really? Whatever your answer, your emotions are at the heart of who you are—of your authentic self. By ignoring or denying any of them, you are ignoring or denying those parts of you. If you don't know what you are feeling, you don't know that essential part of you. Ultimately, you must know and value *all* of your emotions—even the painful ones—to feel at home in your *self*.

The exercises in this chapter encourage you to explore and develop a healthier relationship with your emotions. On the one hand, you might discover emotions you never knew were there, or that were so on the periphery of your awareness that they were more like shadowy figures in your life than obvious players. On the other hand, you might learn that your emotions can sometimes so overpower your thinking that you remain committed to your emotionally driven decisions…even when rational explanations "prove" that your actions are problematic. For example, Lindsey returned to that no-good ex of hers even when she agreed with her friends' cautions about how he would hurt her again. While your emotions cannot be wrong—they just… are—they can cause you unnecessary suffering and influence you to make poor decisions.

By completing the exercises in this chapter, you will learn to identify, tolerate, accept, and appreciate your emotions. This will set you on a path of developing more secure relationships with yourself and others. While the exercises can't possibly teach you all there is to learn about your emotions, they do provide an excellent launching pad for a journey of emotional self-discovery.

Identifying Your Emotions

Is it sometimes hard to know what you are feeling? The truth is that identifying emotions can be unexpectedly difficult for anyone. Some reasons for this are that people often have:

- *A number of emotions at once.* When this happens, it may be hard to identify what you feel.

- *Conflicting emotions.* For example, you can feel both angry and loving toward the same person. When this happens, we often also feel confused or at least a sense of tension from that conflict.

- *Difficulty distinguishing emotions from thoughts.* It's not unusual for someone to say that they feel they have nothing to offer a relationship, when, in fact, this is a thought that may accompany feeling inadequate. By failing to make the distinction, you may remain out of touch with your emotions and unable to explore them further.

- *Emotions that combine with thoughts to create emotional thoughts.* For example, feelings of betrayal after a partner has an affair are a combination of hurt, anger, and thoughts about the situation.

Identifying your emotions not only increases your self-awareness but also requires that you step out of the experience long enough to label them. This process lessens the intensity of your emotions, even if only briefly, before you slip back into experiencing them. At times when your emotions become more intense, you can consciously focus on labeling them as a way to have them without being overpowered.

Your ultimate goal for labeling emotions is to gain mindful acceptance of them, enabling you to feel truly at home in your emotional and multidimensional self. When you can do this, you will also be better able to navigate emotionally upsetting situations and to communicate effectively with your partner (and others) about emotional topics.

Label Your Emotions

Practice labeling your emotions by first thinking about an emotionally upsetting situation. Briefly describe it here:

_____

_____

_____

Bring the situation to mind enough that it stirs up your emotions. Read the following list of emotions and circle all of the emotions that you feel in this circumstance. (This is a full list of emotions that you may want to refer to in the future. For now, you can scroll past the positive emotions to the ones that are likely to fit.)

Emotions Checklist

Happy

At ease	Comfortable	Playful	Joyful	Optimistic
Spirited	Satisfied	Cheerful	Grateful	Proud
Wonderful	Pleased	Inspired	Calm	Alive
Hopeful	Blissful	Lighthearted	Serene	Awe
Energetic	Well-Being	Glad	Elated	Content
Peaceful	Excited	Relaxed	Exhilarated	Delighted
Ecstatic	Humorous	Thankful		

Secure

Adept	Composed	Inspired	Cocky	Worthy
Capable	Condescending	Savvy	Together	Brave
Independent	Privileged	Thoughtful	Competent	Affirmed
Lovable	Strong	Successful	Important	Appeased
Self-reliant	Arrogant	Courageous	Invulnerable	Forgiven
Adequate	Confident	Invincible	Self-Assured	Redeemed
Relieved	Vindicated			

Loved

Accepted	Desired	Revered	Favored	Idolized
Belonging	Admired	Wanted	Understood	Validated
Included	Cherished	Adored	Appreciated	
Respected	Valued	Desirable		

Loving

Affectionate	Adoring	Infatuated	Concerned	Warm
Attracted	Desirous	Forgiving	Empathic	Yearning
Fond	Lustful	Caring	Tender	Enchanted
Longing	Trusting	Compassionate	Liking	Connected

Interested

Absorbed	Intrigued	Fervent	Engrossed	Dedicated
Challenged	Addicted	Motivated	Focused	Compelled
Determined	Committed	Anticipating	Resolute	Enthusiastic
Fascinated	Eager	Curious	Ardent	Intent
Passionate				

Unhappy

Agonized	Disheartened	Lonely	Sad	Needy
Discontented	Down	Regretful	Despondent	Dismayed
Hurt	Confused	Tortured	Worn down	Despairing
Negative	Sullen	Dark	Remorseful	Dissatisfied
Anguished	Blue	Melancholy	Miserable	Gloomy
Alone	Pessimistic	Low	Detached	Heartbroken
Discouraged	Defeated	Empty	Moody	Depressed
Pained	Depleted	Withdrawn	Disappointed	Somber
Stubborn	Hopeless	Stressed	Disorganized	Helpless
Rushed	Overwhelmed	Pressured	Burdened	Grief ridden
Worn out	Devastated	Powerless	Guilty	

Insecure

Awkward	Baffled	Bewildered	Impotent	Ashamed
Inferior	Disoriented	Embarrassed	Foolish	Inadequate
Indecisive	Lost	Puzzled	Silly	Invisible
Weak	Torn	Uncertain	Uneasy	Jealous
Uncomfortable	Pathetic	Unsure	Worthless	Envious
Useless	Unlovable	Insignificant	Repulsive	Fragile

Unloved

Abandoned	Misunderstood	Discarded	Victimized	Shamed
Criticized	Rejected	Disrespected	Betrayed	Isolated
Hated	Alienated	Overlooked	Disparaged	Vulnerable
Lonely	Deserted	Used	Labeled	Alone
Singled out	Ignored	Belittled	Humiliated	Ridiculed
Aching	Oppressed	Disgraced	Chastised	Excluded
Cut off	Unsupported	Judged		

Afraid

Suspicious	Defenseless	Horrified	Shaky	Concerned
Cowardly	Hesitant	Scared	Worried	Exposed
Trapped	Petrified	Threatened	Cautious	Panicked
Paranoid	Timid	Apprehensive	Dreading	Tense
Terrified	Anxious	Doubtful	Nervous	Persecuted
Alarmed	Distrustful	Hysterical		

Angry

Aggressive	Detesting	Hostile	Livid	Scornful
Defiant	Furious	Irritated	Resentful	Incensed
Disapproving	Irate	Despising	Contemptuous	Provoked
Mad	Outraged	Bitter	Frustrated	Dismissive
Offended	Critical	Loathing	Indignant	Deploring
Annoyed	Hating			

Disgusted

Repelled	Repulsed	Appalled	Revolted	Nauseated
Disdainful				

Indifferent

Ambivalent	Apathetic	Bored	Unfocused	Complacent
Flat	Lackadaisical	Numb	Distant	Lethargic
Lazy	Unmotivated	Passive		

Surprised

Amazed	Astonished	Shocked	Startled	Disillusioned
Perplexed				

Write about each emotion that you circled, or focus on ones that feel particularly powerful. What is prompting each emotion? How do these different emotions relate to each other? The more fully you describe your experience, the more you are nurturing greater self-awareness, which can help with having empathy for yourself and ultimately compassionate self-awareness.

_____

_____

_____

_____

_____

You might find that repeating this exercise for different situations, positive and negative, adds to your insights. You can access this checklist of emotions online at https://drbecker-phelps.com/insecure-in-love-workbook or at http://www.newharbinger.com/52175. Each evening, or whenever you think it would help, use the list to identify the emotions you felt during the day. You might also want to journal about your emotions to explore them further or practice sharing them with your partner, or a trusted friend, which can help you deepen your relationship. You can also return to this exercise after you have increased your emotional self-awareness by completing more of the exercises in this chapter.

Sit Mindfully with Your Emotions

Rather than picking your emotions apart like some puzzle to be solved, or just riding them like the Tilt-a-Whirl at a carnival, you can learn to consciously observe and experience them with mindful awareness. By doing this, you can feel at home with them—and with yourself. Begin this exercise by identifying an emotional situation that taps your attachment insecurity.

_____

_____

Read through the directions that follow. Then, sitting quietly with your eyes closed or your gaze down, follow them. Or, if you prefer, you can access a recording of the directions online at https://drbecker-phelps .com/insecure-in-love-workbook or at http://www.newharbinger.com/52175.

Focus on your breath. If you are particularly distressed, concentrating on breathing can help to calm and ground you.

Reflect on your chosen situation make own entry in list. Remember what happened with as much detail as you can—noting what you saw, heard, smelled, or even tasted in the situation. Be aware of any sensations, thoughts, emotions, or actions taken by you or another person.

Bring awareness to your bodily sensations. As you notice them, attend to whatever emotions they seem to be expressing.

Label your emotions. You are not trying to figure them out. Rather, you are just naming the experiences. Like learning a person's name when you first meet them, it's an opening to get to know them better. If multiple emotions have essentially melded into a single massive boulder of distress, a bit of patience can go a long way toward enabling you to separate them.

Sit with one emotion. Getting to know your emotions requires being *with* them, not just thinking *about* them. Choose one emotion to attend to. Sit with it like you might sit quietly with a friend. When you become distracted, which will happen, acknowledge this, and then refocus on your emotion. This can be particularly challenging with painful emotions, so be gentle with yourself.

While a little discomfort can facilitate growth, too much can set you back or even be traumatizing. So, if you overreach, consciously calm yourself. You might do this by simply returning to a few mindful breaths and mentally stepping back from the situation. Then you can return to being *with* your emotion. This process can help you increase your tolerance.

Return awareness to your surroundings. When the intensity of your emotion dissipates, or if it remains too strong, or when you just feel you are ready to move on, shift your focus to your body's seated position. Then open your eyes and look around, to take in the room. If you continue to feel distressed, you might find it helpful to engage in any of the comforting activities you identified in "How to Soothe Your Nervous System" in chapter 3.

Now it is time for some reflection. Was it difficult to name your emotions? What was your experience of trying to stay with your chosen emotion? In what ways did the emotion change as you attended to it? How well were you able to stay with the emotion without being overcome by it? Do you have any other insights?

_____

_____

_____

_____

_____

_____

There is so much to consider here that you might want to continue writing your thoughts in your journal.

Sitting mindfully with your emotions is an exercise that you can benefit from practicing in different situations, especially ones that you find emotionally challenging. The more you practice being with your emotions, the more you will be able to tolerate and then befriend them. Even painful emotions like grief can become welcome emotions. They will feel "right" even when they don't feel "good." As a result of accepting all of your emotions, you will feel more whole.

Protests and Your Emotions

If you often protest against abandonment, you can benefit from gaining more emotional self-awareness around this dynamic. Use the emotions checklist in the last section (or print the online one) to help you complete this exercise.

Review the "Do You Protest Abandonment?" exercise in chapter 2, including examples you provided. The types of abandonment named in that section are listed on the left in the following chart. In the column on the right, label the emotions you feel for each way you protest. There will be overlap, but you might also notice some different emotions in the different types of protesting. For example, "being needy" might be accompanied by feeling impotent, which you might not feel while "playing games."

Protest	Emotions
Frequently seeking emotional reassurance:	
Frequently seeking help with tasks:	
Frequently reestablishing communication:	
Needing a lot of physical reassurance:	
"Playing games":	
Responding angrily:	
Being highly people-pleasing:	
Falling into despair:	

Note any thoughts or insights you have about the emotions you experience with your protest behaviors. Do particular emotions accompany most or all protests? Considering each emotion, does it arise before, during, or after the protest? How do your protest behaviors affect the intensity of your emotions?

_____

_____

_____

_____

_____

Reflect on situations in which your protests worked to get your partner's attention and caring. Before, during, and after you received their attention, consider: How did you feel toward your partner? How did you feel about yourself? Did the reassurance ultimately strengthen your sense of security or did it only comfort you in the moment?

_____

_____

_____

_____

_____

If you have more to say in response to the previous two prompts, continue writing about them in your journal.

As discussed in chapter 2, your tendency to protest rejection likely began in childhood. The next section will help you explore this further. (In chapter 7, you will be able to deepen your self-awareness related to protest behaviors by reflecting more on how they affect your current relationship.)

Reflect and Connect

You can gain a greater understanding of your current anxious attachment style by reflecting back on early protest behaviors.

For example, as Jennifer identified the ways in which she protested her partner rejecting her and the emotions that accompanied those behaviors, she recalled similar experiences as a child. She realized that she protested rejection back then by being emotionally needy, _always_ working to excel as a student and soccer player so that she could earn approval from her parents, teachers, coach, and peers. She also protested by constantly reestablishing communication with others in the hope of them reassuring her of her value. But even when people expressed their approval, it only felt good for a moment. Then she quickly returned to having that gnawing sense that she was not good enough. Though she did not realize it as a child, she can see now that she was trying desperately to escape from feeling lonely, insecure, and anxious. In reflecting on all of this, it became crystal clear how she has repeated these early dynamics in her romantic relationships.

To gain more insight into your anxious attachment style, turn to your notes from the previous "Protests and Your Emotions" exercise. Review them. Then think back to your childhood. Can you remember times when you felt the same insecurity-related emotions and enacted the protests that you see in your life now? Describe a few of these events and your accompanying emotions from the perspective of your child self.

_____

_____

_____

_____

_____

Now view these events from a caring, adult perspective. If this proves too difficult, try imagining another child in these situations. Then apply that perspective to yourself. Do your best to understand what caused you to feel as you did. For example, Cody knows he is hard on himself, always feeling inferior to his current partner. He easily traced this back to his childhood when he felt misunderstood at home and was outside of all friend groups. Although he has a lot of good friends now, the old *you'll be alone forever* voice continues to haunt him and leave him feeling fearful, lonely, inadequate, and despairing.

How do attachment-related anxieties from your past often replay in your life now, even when they don't really fit a current situation? Use the space here to explore any insights about this.

_____

_____

_____

_____

_____

_____

Take time to reflect on what you've written. You might also find it helpful to talk with a caring friend or your therapist. As new insights emerge, write about them in your journal, or talk again with someone supportive. This process can nurture compassionate self-awareness, which can then open you to feeling more secure in yourself and your relationships.

Rate the Intensity of Your Emotions

Rating the intensity of your emotions can help you get to know them better. Also, by identifying when they are beginning to overtake your thinking, you can preemptively calm them, similar to what you did with the exercise "Rating Your Levels of Arousal" in chapter 3.

Get started by picking an emotion you would like to rate, such as anger, fear, or even happiness. Use the scale provided here. First, write your chosen emotion at the top. Using the scale line below it, label the tick mark at the left endpoint with the least intense form of that emotion and the one at the right endpoint with the most intense form. Then place tick marks along the scale, labeling your emotions at increasing levels of intensity, using your sensations, thoughts, and actions to help to clarify them.

Here's an example of an intensity scale that's partly completed for the emotion of fear (in this case, fear of judgment):

Emotion: Fear

- Shoulders tense
- Note something's wrong

- Preoccupied with possible disaster
- Heart beating fast

Uncomfortable

- A little restless
- May not notice

Anxious

- Fidgety
- Worried thoughts
- Talk more

Terrified

- Mind blank
- Shallow breathing
- Body Tense

Emotion: _____

- _____
- _____

- _____
- _____

_____

- _____
- _____
- _____

_____

- _____
- _____
- _____

_____

- _____
- _____
- _____

Identify the point on your scale at which you begin not being able to think clearly. Circle that level of emotional intensity. List things you can do to calm yourself when you feel the level of intensity just before the circled emotion. To help, check out the activities you identified in "How to Soothe Your Nervous System" in chapter 3.

_____

_____

_____

_____

Practice attending to your chosen emotion and its different levels of intensity in daily life. This alone might help you calm down or respond in healthier ways. For example, rather than screaming in fury at your partner, you might recognize when you are annoyed and talk constructively with them instead. Or, rather than lending money to a new love when you feel giddy with happiness, you might recognize this as a time when you need to be cautious about following your heart. If you have a sense that your emotional thinking may be leading you astray, pause and journal about the situation or talk with a supportive friend.

Identifying the Patterns of Your Emotional Reactions

Have you ever been embarrassed by your jealousy? Or felt afraid of your own anger? Having emotional reactions to emotions happens all the time. You have an initial *primary emotion*, which you react to with a *secondary emotion* as a way to avoid the pain of your first reaction. For example, if you and your partner agree to split, your sadness, loneliness, and grief are primary emotions. Then you might react to those emotions with the secondary emotion of anger toward yourself for being so upset, despite practically screaming in your own head, *He's so not worth it!* In the end, you become a hot mess. You struggle with the secondary emotions *and* your primary emotions, even if you don't realize that the primary emotions are still there.

In addition, both levels of emotions are often affected by your attachment style. For example, as an anxiously attached person who questions his worth, Scott was constantly on his best behavior and doing favors for his partner, Alex, who was always caring toward him. With some self-reflection, Scott realized that he was over-the-top helpful as a way to prevent (or protest against) being rejected. Like so many anxiously attached people, he was often gripped by a fear of rejection, even when others treated him well. So, in the situation with Alex, Scott's primary emotion of fear was maladaptive, and it interfered with Scott and Alex developing a truly emotionally close relationship. To make matters worse, Scott responded to this maladaptive primary emotion by becoming angry with himself (secondary emotion), which undermined his relationship with himself.

Identify an Emotion That Replays in Your Life

To help you identify a (likely maladaptive) primary emotion and a secondary emotion, reflect on your life and name one emotion that seems to replay. It might be shame, anger, anxiety, fear, or something else. Write it here: _____

Recall three situations in which you felt this emotion. For each one, complete the columns in the chart, as follows:

Situation: Describe the events and important aspects of the situation that you were reacting to.

Initial emotional reaction: In addition to the basic emotion that you already named, describe other aspects of it (such as its intensity) or other related emotions. Then sit with your emotions, much as you did in the "Sit Mindfully with Your Emotions" exercise earlier in this chapter.

Emotions after sitting: Describe other emotions that emerged as you were open to them.

You can get a sense of the way this works by looking at how Bill, who struggles with anger, filled out the first row of this chart.

Situation	Initial Emotional Reaction (*primary emotions*)	Emotions After Sitting (*secondary emotions*)
Example: Mike would not listen to my good advice about how to plan for our vacation, and instead he ended up paying more for plane tickets and made reservations at a hotel that I'm sure will be a disappointment.	Quick to anger, furious, disrespected	Sad, alone, invisible, deflated, not valued

Situation	Initial Emotional Reaction (*primary emotions*)	Emotions After Sitting (*secondary emotions*)

After completing the chart with three different situations, look at the patterns of emotions and name the ones that emerge:

Primary emotion(s): _____

Secondary emotion(s): _____

What might be motivating you to turn to the secondary emotion(s) rather than staying with your primary one(s)? Is your primary emotion a maladaptive one? If so, review the "Reflect and Connect" section earlier in this chapter and describe how you think you developed this maladaptive pattern.

_____

_____

_____

_____

_____

This chapter encourages you to develop a lifelong relationship with your emotions that is respectful and curious. To help achieve that goal, repeat these exercises or just continue to explore your emotions in less structured ways. With these efforts, you will continue to grow and develop a healthier, more intimate relationship with your ever-evolving self.

CHAPTER 7

STEAM: Actions

From simple tasks like your morning routine to how you manage your career and personal life, the actions you take every day are affected by your attachment style. For instance, think about your choice of clothes for today or any day. Do you dress in less-than-fashionable clothes or in dark colors as an expression of your sense of having little worth (model of self)? Or do you dress this way in an effort—perhaps unconscious—to avoid negative attention and possible judgment from others (model of others)? On the other hand, you might dress stylishly or in bright colors in an effort to feel better about yourself and to win the approval of a potential partner.

As you can see, to understand yourself, it's important to be aware of your actions as well as your motivations. In addition, by increasing awareness of what is influencing your actions, how they affect responses from others, and how they more generally affect your life, you can open yourself to healing through compassionate self-awareness and to making new, healthier choices, including nurturing a secure love relationship.

Assessing Nonverbal Communication

By becoming more consciously aware of nonverbal cues, you can learn to recognize and reconsider the messages you are sending and receiving. With this in mind, briefly describe an interaction with a date or partner in which you felt insecure.

_____

_____

_____

_____

Next, describe how the following types of nonverbal communication from both you and the other person played a part in the interaction. Consider how you interpret such nonverbal communication. Are you aware of a tendency to see disinterest or rejection where it does not exist or to perceive it as bigger than it is? Are you taking the context of the situation or the temperament of the other person into account?

Prosody: This is the pattern and rhythm of speech, such as the volume, pitch, and tempo. It also includes the emotional tone, such as being gentle, excited, strident, condescending, or threatening. These cues suggest the emotional state of the speaker and indicate their thinking and the next actions they might take. Depending upon your perception of prosody, the same words, such as "Yeah, I love you," can be a source of comfort or a trigger for being consumed by a sense of rejection.

_____

_____

_____

_____

_____

Posture: When people stand in an upright posture with shoulders back, they are physically grounded and stable in their bodies. It tends to communicate self-assurance. However, when the body is held rigidly and movements are not smooth, a person can appear highly anxious. You might notice that your torso tends to slouch when you feel dismissed or defeated. Sometimes when people notice someone else has good posture, they become more self-conscious and feel more inadequate, perhaps even imagining that they are being judged.

_____

_____

_____

_____

_____

Body placement: Where you are physically in relation to someone else can say a lot. If you are dating someone who stands and sits close to you, they are likely showing romantic interest. On the other hand, if they give you plenty of personal space, that distance may indicate that they would never want greater closeness, or don't want it yet. Or it could indicate that they are shy or unsure of how you feel. So you need to be careful in interpreting this.

_____

_____

_____

_____

_____

Physical reactions: Many involuntary physical reactions can be observed. People's faces often turn red when they are embarrassed or angry. Their bodies sometimes shake when they are afraid. And their breathing is often constrained when they are anxious and fearful of rejection.

_____

_____

_____

_____

_____

Gestures: People often communicate with gestures rather than words, such as when someone holds your hand to show they feel connected to you. However, as with verbal communication, you must understand gestures in their context. Not holding your hand might indicate lack of interest in a romantic relationship or not liking PDA (public displays of affection).

_____

_____

_____

_____

_____

Eye contact: Maintaining eye contact is often used to intensify an experience. When people feel loving, holding eye contact expresses greater emotional closeness. However, when linked with being angry, it can be threatening. By contrast, avoiding eye contact generally increases emotional distance. People may avoid eye contact when they are lying or when they are uncomfortable with closeness for other reasons, such as fear of being judged. Or, lack of eye contact may have nothing to do with anything interpersonal; someone may simply be distracted by the lights of a police car in the distance.

_____

_____

_____

_____

_____

_____

If you found this exercise enlightening, you might want to repeat it in your journal. With practice, you can become more adept at noticing the role of nonverbal communication in your relationships.

How Do You Protest Abandonment?

As you may remember from chapter 2, people first use protests during childhood in an attempt to protect against being rejected or abandoned, and they often continue to use such protests throughout their lives. In chapter 6, you explored the emotions that accompany your protests. Now it's time to learn more about your protest behaviors by thinking about how they affect your relationships.

Listed below are the types of protest behaviors that were introduced in the "Do You Protest Abandonment?" exercise in chapter 2. For each type of protest that you acknowledged using, refer to the example that you provided, and then write down how the other person responded to your protest and how it affected your relationship in the short term and in the long term. To illustrate, here's an example for the protest of frequently seeking emotional reassurance: *Sue's partner initially responded to her nearly daily emotional crises with gentle caring, but eventually distanced herself because offering this support so often was too draining.*

Frequently seeking emotional reassurance:

_____

_____

_____

_____

Frequently seeking help with tasks as a way to stay close:

_____

_____

_____

_____

Frequently reestablishing communication (such as repeatedly reaching out by text or phone or looking for ways to "accidentally" run into your partner):

_____

_____

_____

_____

Needing a lot of physical reassurance (such as hugs, kisses, sex):

_____

_____

_____

_____

"Playing games" to try to reengage your partner (such as pretending to have an admirer):

_____

_____

_____

_____

Responding angrily, hoping that your partner will try to appease you and reconnect:

_____

_____

_____

_____

Being highly people-pleasing (also known as the please-and-appease or fawning reaction, in which you overlook your wants and needs to meet the wants, needs, and wishes of your partner):

_____

_____

_____

_____

Falling into despair, giving up and losing hope that you can connect with your partner (when you are no longer protesting):

_____

_____

_____

Now consider the overall effects on your relationships of using these protests. Protests sometimes create distance in relationships instead of eliciting reassurance. Have you noticed this pattern? If so, describe how the dynamic has tended to unfold:

_____

_____

_____

_____

_____

_____

Many people find that being reassured by their partner helps in the moment, but they quickly return to fearing rejection and protesting again. If you can relate to this, write about your experience:

_____

_____

_____

_____

_____

Do you notice any other patterns? Do you have any particular insights?

_____

_____

_____

_____

_____

_____

While observing problematic patterns of protesting won't immediately stop them, it offers a chance to address any issues in the moment and increases the likelihood that you will respond in healthier ways in the future.

Observe Your Reaction to Physical Affection

Have you noticed that despite really wanting to feel loved, you avoid or outright reject other people's attempts to show you affection or to comfort you? Rather than seeking out your partner when you are upset, you might skulk off to hide in your bed. Even you may not fully understand why. But there is a good reason for it. To take in comfort or affection, you must lower your defenses. This would make you vulnerable to getting hurt—something you have learned to reflexively avoid. It's a real conundrum. So, what can you do?

Many people try to force themselves to open up. You can do this, but chances are that you would feel like a victim to your own pressure, which would actually make matters worse. Instead, learn to respect your need to protect yourself. Also, develop compassion for your struggles by learning to understand your reactions. This will reinforce your model of self as someone whose experience is to be valued and respected. From this emotionally safe position, you are more likely to feel okay about questioning your defensive reactions. Then you might slowly open up to taking in comfort from people you judge to be truly caring and supportive. This is all much easier said than done, but this next exercise encourages you to develop such a self-accepting perspective.

Rate Your Openness to Physical Affection

Begin by reflecting on your experience of being hugged by someone you love. If you need to jog your memory, actually hug someone you love and pay attention to your sensations, thoughts, and emotions. Then complete the following brief questionnaire:

Rate each statement on a scale of 1 to 5, with 1 being not at all and 5 being very much. Then add up your ratings for a total.

_____   I sense caring *from* the other person.

_____   I feel caring *for* the other person.

_____   I feel emotionally comforted by the hug.

_____   The hug helps physically calm my body.

_____   Total

What does your total rating mean? Understanding that the lowest total score you can get is 4, the lower your score is, the less open you are to absorbing the love offered. Are certain scores higher or lower than the rest? If so, what are they saying about you and your openness to physical affection and emotional acceptance? For instance, you might rate the statements about being comforted or calmed by a hug lower than the other statements, perhaps reflecting a difficulty in emotionally taking in a hug despite registering it as a message of caring.

_____

_____

_____

_____

Would you respond differently to different people? If you think your response depends on who's hugging you, you might try repeating the questionnaire for different people. Then look for themes. For instance, some people are very open to receiving physical comfort from women but not from men, or from children but not from adults. _____

_____

_____

_____

What are some implications of this exercise? How does your level of openness to physical affection influence your sense of feeling cared about or alone in the world? How does it affect your relationship? How might your relationship be different if you were more open to truly receiving affection? Reflect on the different themes that you notice.

_____

_____

_____

_____

_____

_____

_____

After completing this exercise, when someone hugs you, consciously choose to be open to the caring they offer as well as to the physical warmth. If you try to take in a hug but don't feel comforted, it's okay. That's your starting point. You can continue to be aware of your experiences when you hug. Feeling the warmth may come with time and with the other inner work that you are doing.

Are You Trying Too Hard?

Are you pouring your heart into doing things that drain you much more than they energize you? And is slowing down out of the question because you think it would mean you are falling short and would reveal to everyone (including yourself) that you are inadequate…and this would lead to them dismissing, abandoning, or rejecting you?

If you were nodding while reading those questions, then pay close attention: *You do not need to live like this.* There are people with a positive self-image who choose not to put 110 percent into everything they do and especially not into things that ultimately pull them down. They acknowledge having limitations and respect them. Though they try hard, at times even pushing their limits, they don't live in a state of chronic total or near depletion. And importantly, if others don't like their decisions, they can still feel good about themselves. This allows them to live a more balanced life. No, I am not making this up. And you can grow into this version of yourself, too!

Assessing How You Manage Relationships

With all this in mind, it's important to assess whether there are aspects of your life that take such a toll on you that they interfere with you experiencing pleasure and feeling secure in yourself. Start by identifying something you are working extremely hard at, such as advancing at work or helping out a friend.

_____

_____

_____

Create a pros and cons list. Include everything you can think of, and be specific. If you tend to motivate yourself through self-criticism, the cons list will likely also include things like chronic self-doubt, fear of judgment, and unhappiness despite successes at what you've been working on. Here's an example: *Being Julia's girlfriend.*

Pros	Cons
Feel like a good girlfriend Enjoy helping Like her company	Feel taken advantage of. She expects me to always be there for her and to help her whenever she asks (which is often). Interferes with plans with other friends (always cancel plans with them when she asks). Interferes with reading and other things I like to do. Always afraid she will be angry with me if I say no.

Now look your own pros and cons:

Pros	Cons

Reflect on your list. Think about what your pros and cons tell you when you consider them together. Overall, does pouring so much effort into this aspect of your life make you happy or fulfilled? If you tend to justify current unhappiness with the idea that you are making sacrifices for the future, think hard about this investment. How likely (and when) will your actions lead to a sense of fulfillment? If you are ultimately outwardly successful, will you also eventually feel appreciated for who you are? Or will you need to continue working hard because you only feel appreciated for what you do? Example of being Julia's girlfriend: As much as I enjoy being in a relationship with Julia, it is taking over my life. I used to think Julia would see what a good girlfriend I am and would become less demanding and appreciate me more. I also thought she'd be there for me. I'm not so sure that's going to happen. She does some nice things for me, but I don't feel like she's really there for me like I'm there for her. I am angry with her, which makes me feel guilty and selfish. I also don't want her to be angry with me. It's hard to say, but I don't think this relationship is worth all the effort I'm putting in.

Now it's your turn to reflect on your list:

_____

_____

_____

_____

_____

_____

If you assess that your hard work is worth it, then you are done with the exercise for now. You might reassess this area at another time. Or, you might use your journal to do the exercise again for another area of your life. However, if you think that you are putting in too much effort, then continue on.

Formulate an alternative approach to a balanced life with two steps. The first step is to *identify your needs*. Ask yourself, how do you (or can you) try to meet them? For example, Julia's girlfriend identified her needs: Maintaining a relationship is really important to me. I want to keep our relationship, and I really want Julia to like me. Then she asked herself how she tries to meet those needs: I do this by caring about her and helping out when she asks.

Now identify your needs:

_____

_____

_____

How do you (or can you) try to meet them?

_____

_____

_____

The second step is to *identify your limitations*. Ask yourself, *How can you work within them and what are the benefits of doing this?* Julia's girlfriend identified these limitations: No matter what I do, I cannot control whether she likes me or is happy with me. Also, I only have so many hours in a day. If I am available whenever she wants me, I lose out on other important people and things in my life.

How to work within limitations: Continue to be in a relationship with Julia. Do things with her when I want to. Help her out when she asks. Do not cancel other plans when she asks for help. And do not delay making plans with others when she's tentative about making plans. Too often, I think I'm her backup plan. She decides to do something else, and I end up alone with nothing to do.

Benefits of working within limitations: By doing this, I will be doing all I can to keep our relationship, but I won't be putting myself in the position of feeling like a doormat. Hopefully, it will work. If she does get upset with me and pulls away, then I will be sad, but I can spend more time with people who really appreciate me.

Now it's your turn to identify your limitations:

_____

_____

_____

How can you work within these limitations?

_____

_____

_____

_____

What are the benefits of doing this?

_____

_____

_____

_____

When you are setting boundaries, sometimes self-doubt, relationship problems, or issues related to feeling judged will arise. It's important that you support and encourage yourself, as you would do for a friend. It might help to recognize that you would not think less of a colleague or a friend who held firm to accepting their limitations so that they could lead a more balanced life.

If you alter your behavior based on your observations and reflections, great. If not, that's okay. It can be really difficult to change behavioral patterns. For this reason, it's good to focus on understanding the benefits of respecting your needs and limits. The actual change may come later, along with other efforts you are making in this workbook. To gain even greater awareness and appreciation of your actions and how they affect your relationships, you might find it helpful to write in your journal about ongoing observations and reflections.

Observe How You Find Meaning in Life

To help you realize that you are more than your insecurities, think about the things you do that feel good to engage in and that give you a sense of meaning and purpose. Consider what those activities are by making notes on them in the following aspects of your life:

Work (such as learning new skills, facing fears, helping others…):

_____

_____

_____

Hobbies (reading, designing homemade birthday cards, playing computer games...):

_____

_____

_____

Connecting with something larger (praying, joining a political movement, communing with nature...):

_____

_____

_____

Volunteering (working in a food bank, fostering dogs, being a Big Brother or Big Sister...):

_____

_____

_____

_____

Social connections (lunch with friends, playing in a weekly card game, helping your child or an aging parent...):

_____

_____

_____

When you engage in any of these activities, in what ways do you feel even a little better about yourself? Do you feel at all more open to others seeing you more positively? In addition to making some notes here, consider writing more about this in your journal, including making a plan to do more.

_____

_____

_____

_____

_____

List any of these activities that might help to calm and ground you when you are upset. (You might want to add these to your coping skills in the exercise "List Go-To Activities to Calm Your Distress.")

_____

_____

_____

As you become more aware of your actions and what they communicate to yourself and others, you may find that you can choose to act differently. Even if you don't change how you behave, you may develop new insights about yourself. This awareness can work in combination with the other domains of STEAM to help you have a richer appreciation of yourself. We will address bringing together these different areas of awareness in the next chapter on mentalizing.

CHAPTER 8

STEAM: Mentalizing

Can you intellectually understand why you act as you do? Can you emotionally connect with your inner experiences? If you really do "get" where you are coming from, then you are *mentalizing* yourself. As a result, you are more likely to be able to relate to yourself with empathy, compassion, and forgiveness. These are signs of having a healthy relationship with yourself. To this point in the workbook, we have focused on self-awareness, which is the foundation of being able to mentalize yourself. But such self-focus alone is insufficient for nurturing a healthy relationship with someone else. There are, after all, two of you. So it is also essential that you have *other*-awareness and that you mentalize your partner, too.

Mentalizing is something that you do every day without consciously thinking about it. For example, can you remember a time when you were struggling and instinctively picked up the phone to call a close friend? Can you remember a time when you held the door for someone else because you assumed they would appreciate the gesture? These situations reveal a natural appreciation of what is going on within you and another person.

Along with such effortless (or near effortless) everyday mentalizing, there are many situations which require more conscious mentalizing. For instance, Barbara was surprised and frustrated when Eric got angry with her for offering ideas about improving his work situation. By putting her emotions aside long enough to listen to Eric's explanation of feeling judged by her unsolicited advice, she was able to mentalize him: understanding, empathizing, and having compassion for him. With that, she offered a heartfelt apology, and the tension between them was alleviated. Situations like this, where there is a miscommunication, often require conscious effort to mentalize. Can you think of a circumstance in which you were able to resolve a conflict by taking the time to understand and connect with another person's perspective?

If you often have trouble mentalizing yourself or others, then you are far from alone. Mentalizing can be really difficult to do, especially when you are feeling particularly emotional. Fortunately, mentalizing is a skill that you can strengthen by attending to the interconnected domains of experience (STEA). As your self-awareness in each of these domains increases, you can consciously weave them together to enrich your self-understanding and develop compassionate self-awareness. Also, this increasing self-awareness can help you to be more open to the experiences of others. As a result, you can develop compassionate other-awareness. Altogether, this process can naturally help heal insecurity within yourself and in your relationships as you nurture more secure attachment.

Assessing Your Reaction in Context

Failing to maintain healthy habits can lead to impaired mentalizing. For example, think about times when you have struggled with not getting enough sleep. Did you notice that it was harder to think clearly and you were more easily frustrated? By definition, this means that it was also harder to mentalize.

The "Taking Care of the Basics" exercise in chapter 3 encouraged you to identify a weakness in, and to work on, any of these eleven basic factors in a healthy lifestyle. Given that problems in any of these factors may impair your ability to mentalize, consider them again now. Check off the ones that you think you have recently struggled to achieve or to maintain and that have also been making it more difficult to mentalize yourself or others.

☐ Safe living situation   ☐ Managing finances   ☐ Caring for self when sick

☐ Sufficient sleep   ☐ Healthy eating   ☐ Regular exercise

☐ Maintaining routine   ☐ Strong social connections   ☐ Meaningful activities

☐ Enjoyable activities   ☐ Connection to something larger (e.g., nature, community)

You might want to look back at your answers to the exercise in chapter 3 to see whether your areas of difficulty have changed. What has changed since you completed that activity? How does each area where you have difficulty affect your ability to mentalize yourself and your ability to mentalize others?

_____

_____

_____

_____

_____

Develop a plan to improve in these areas, including getting professional help if that's appropriate.

_____

_____

_____

_____

_____

You may realize that the changes you need to make will take significant effort and focus. If that's the case, use your journal to lay out a more detailed plan and to track your progress, including how your ability to mentalize improves.

Choosing to Be Curious

Curiosity is essential to improving your ability to mentalize yourself and others. However, the quality of your curiosity is key. For example, when you reflect on something you wish you hadn't done, do you tend to be critical, as in, *What's wrong with me that I did that?* Or, are you curious in an engaged (personally invested rather than coldly objective) and nonjudgmental way, as in, *What was going on that I acted like that?* While the first approach will create or reinforce a sense of being flawed in some deep way, the latter can help you feel safe and can open you to empathy and compassion. Similarly, *engaged curiosity* about someone else's experience means being truly open. It is *not* deciding what the person's experience is and then working to prove it. When you approach yourself and others with engaged curiosity, intimate relationships (including with yourself) can bloom.

In this exercise, I encourage you to use engaged curiosity to consciously mentalize yourself and then the other person. Begin by describing a situation with your partner or another person in which you felt insecure. You might choose a circumstance where it is clear that someone was rejecting you, such as them calling you an asshole right to your face. Or, you might choose one that is murkier, such as someone you are dating not calling for a couple of days. Imagine your chosen situation well enough to put yourself back in the experience.

_____

_____

_____

Mentalizing Yourself

Be curious about your own experience. Make notes about each domain of awareness as you attend to it.

Sensations: _____

Thoughts: _____

Emotions: _____

Actions: _____

Describe previous experiences that might be influencing your current one. For example, having been ghosted by someone in the past might lead you to quickly conclude that it's happening again when someone in your current life doesn't immediately respond to your texts.

_____

_____

_____

_____

Consider other possible reactions. Describe how you could have—or how people you know might have—reacted differently in thoughts, emotions, or actions.

_____

_____

_____

_____

Mentalize you. Using what you have observed within yourself, connect with your experience. What prompted your reaction? If you are being self-critical, encourage empathy and self-compassion: can you see how your reaction is a human one that others in your specific circumstance might have? Describe your mentalizing and continue in your journal if necessary.

_____

_____

_____

_____

_____

_____

_____

Mentalizing the Other Person

Be curious about their experience. What do you think the other person experienced in each domain of awareness? Look for outer signs of their inner experiences, such as their gestures, facial expressions, and tone of voice. Trying to figure this out can be tricky, but you can make an educated guess. (If appropriate, you might ask them.) For instance, Dan decided not to approach Hank right after their fight because he could see Hank's breathing was still restricted and his jaw was tightly clenched. He guessed that Hank was experiencing tension in his chest and jaw, feeling anxious, and thinking Dan was going to be critical.

Sensations: _____

Thoughts: _____

Emotions: _____

Actions: _____

Describe anything you know about the other person's previous experiences that might be affecting their current reactions.

_____

_____

_____

_____

Mentalize them. Using what you have observed, try to empathize with the other person's reaction. Can you see how their reaction is a human one that others in this specific circumstance might have? Continue in your journal if necessary.

_____

_____

_____

_____

_____

_____

With your new insights, you might try to repair your relationship.

Keep in mind that having compassion for yourself and your partner does not mean you need to respond in any particular way. For example, after Robin learned to mentalize herself and her husband, she decided to end their marriage. She did not think he was a bad person, but he had a serious drinking problem, and she no longer felt obligated to stay with him given her years of trying to support his recovery.

A Diagram of STEAM

Dr. Paul Ekman (a pioneer in the research of emotions) and the fourteenth Dalai Lama (spiritual leader of Tibet) created an atlas of emotions that can facilitate and clarify your self-awareness. You can explore the atlas of what they've identified as the five universal emotions at http://www.atlasofemotions.org.

I've based the following STEAM diagram on a modification of their work, so as to depict emotional reactions an insecurely attached person might have in response to feeling or fearing rejection, such as anger, sadness, and disgust. Importantly, one possible reaction is to enjoy the relationship even when you fear rejection. Note how the diagram includes all of the domains of STEAM, though mentalizing is not specifically named, because it is what you are doing as you reflect on the other domains.

Importantly, the "Emotional Thoughts" box highlights that emotions tend to bias thinking. However, when people feel emotions, they may also have thoughts that are not emotionally biased. For example, fear can be associated with the emotionally biased thought of *I am going to be rejected* or the more objective thought of *There is a small chance that I could be rejected*. Both kinds of thoughts belong in the "Emotional Thoughts" box.

In addition, the diagram includes three kinds of emotional reactions that were described by Dr. Ekman: *Constructive reactions* help move you toward your goals, such as a when a spouse comforts their distressed partner by being supportive and hugging them. *Destructive reactions* interfere with achieving your goals, such as when a spouse angrily demands that their partner be more loving and supportive. *Ambiguous reactions* are confusing, in that it is unclear whether these reactions will be helpful. An example of this is when a spouse flatly tells their upset partner that everything will be okay.

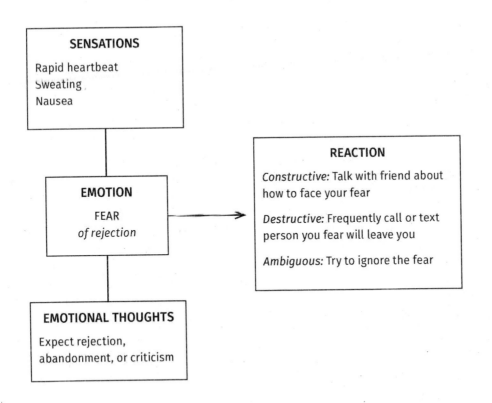

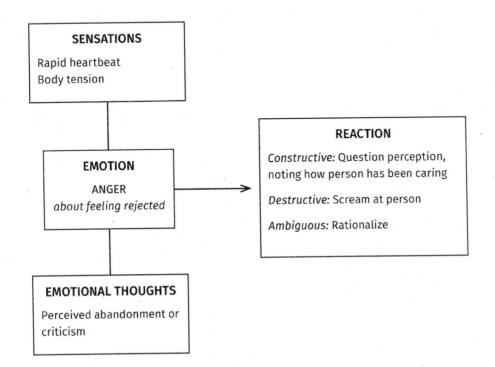

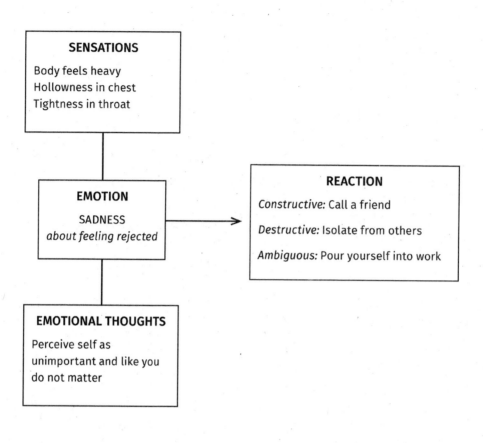

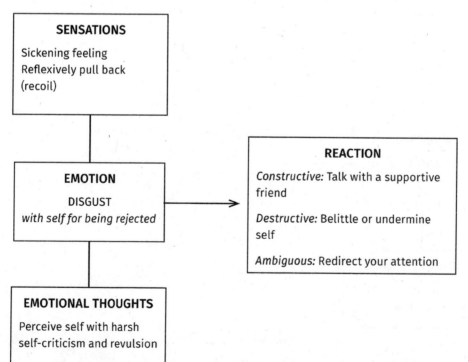

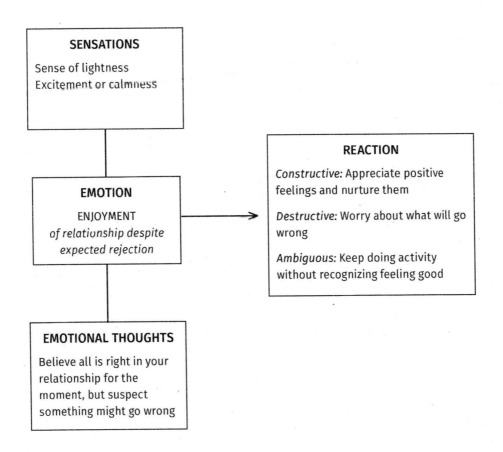

Mapping Your Experiences

In this exercise, you can see how your insecurity *actually* plays out as well as other ways that it *could* play out. Begin by describing a situation in which you felt insecure.

_____

_____

Name the different emotions that you felt. (You may want to consult the emotions checklist from chapter 6.)

_____

_____

Choose one of these emotions to explore. _____

Now complete the STEAM diagram: Fill in the chosen emotion. Next complete the "Sensations" and "Emotional Thoughts" boxes. In the "Reaction" box, write in your actual reaction or reactions, and place a star next to it. Then complete the other possible reactions.

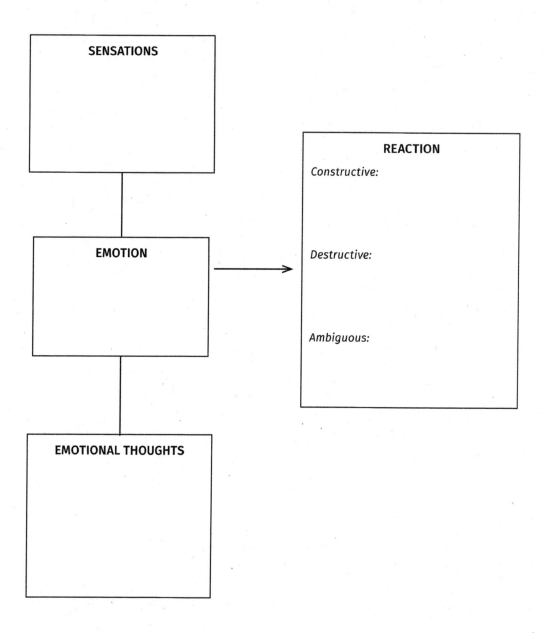

When you have completed the diagram, share your reflections about it here:

_____

_____

_____

_____

_____

_____

You can use the online template at https://drbecker-phelps.com/insecure-in-love-workbook or at http://newharbinger.com/52175 to continue this exercise in three ways:

- Repeat the exercise for other emotions that you identified feeling in the same situation.

- If the reactions box includes new emotions, choose one of them and complete another diagram with that emotion.

- Complete this exercise for different situations.

All of this will help you better understand your patterns of thoughts, emotions, and actions.

Getting to Know Your Partner from the Inside Out

How well do you mentalize your partner? Think about that for a moment. Whatever your response, by working to see the world through their eyes, you can gain a better appreciation of them.

Choose to focus on a personal experience for your partner. Make it one that your partner will want to discuss and that you're open to listening to them talk about. It can be anything from going fishing to mourning the death of their parent. If you feel ready to truly listen (and not argue), you might also choose a topic you disagree about. Write down the topic that you've chosen.

_____

_____

Ask your partner about this topic at a time when you know you will not be interrupted. As you listen, keep the following in mind:

- Give them all of your attention (no multitasking).

- Ask about their thoughts.

- Ask about their feelings.

- Attend to nonverbal cues.

- Try to see the topic from their perspective, even if it differs from yours. (If you think they have the facts wrong, do not correct them. This exercise is about trying to _understand_ their perspective, not correcting it.)

- If they are discussing a problem, don't try to solve it unless they ask you to.

Reflect on their experience. Can you see it through their eyes? Write down what you heard them say about their thoughts and feelings.

_____

_____

_____

_____

_____

_____

_____

Look at what you've written. Is it truly what they communicated to you, or is some of what you wrote an expression of *your* thoughts or feelings? Are there aspects of their experience that you still don't fully understand? If so, asking them follow-up questions might help you understand them better. (That said, if you sense that they don't want to explore the topic further, it is important to respect this, too.)

Write down any insights you have about your attempt to mentalize your partner, what you might do differently next time, and what part of the topic you might want to return to, if appropriate.

_____

_____

_____

_____

_____

_____

_____

With practice, your efforts will pay off. You will understand your partner better, helping you both feel closer to each other. You may also want to follow up on certain topics. That's fine, but be sure not to jump to working on the follow-up before you are able to truly mentalize them and can communicate this understanding to them. This will go a long way toward improving your relationship and alleviating any unnecessary insecurity.

What's in Your Luggage?

Early life experiences help to form how you perceive yourself and others in ways that establish your attachment style. So, let's take a look at what you experienced at a young age and think about how that continues to affect you today. Consider your model of self, which can be anywhere from feeling worthy and lovable to unworthy and unlovable. To help with this, review "Is Your Model of Self Making You Anxious?" in chapter 1.

Note a particular insecure belief you have had about yourself since childhood and the emotions related to it. For instance, you might feel deficient as a person and so feel inadequate, sad, and angry with yourself.

_____

_____

_____

_____

Recall your earliest memories that connect back to this self-perception and any related insecure feelings. For example, Joshua remembers being funny to get attention from family and friends and heading clubs at school to feel accepted there. He senses that he felt empty back then, though he doesn't think he paid much attention to it.

_____

_____

_____

_____

_____

_____

_____

If your memories involve particular people, who are they? If some of those people were outside your home, do you remember having similar feelings with particular family members?

_____

_____

_____

What themes do you notice? In thinking about his life, Joshua realized that while making people laugh made him feel noticed and liked, he never really felt liked just for being himself—not even by his parents.

_____

_____

_____

_____

_____

_____

_____

What did the responses of others or the experiences themselves communicate to you about your value as a person (helping to shape your model of self)?

_____

_____

_____

_____

_____

What did other people "teach" you about others being emotionally available to you (helping to shape your model of others)?

_____

_____

_____

_____

How do you see these early life experiences playing out in your current relationships? Name a recent situation in which you have reacted based on what you "learned" in childhood.

_____

_____

_____

_____

_____

_____

_____

Think about how your insecure attachment experience began at a young age and was reinforced day after day, year after year, becoming a part of who you are. Hopefully this awareness can help you develop self-compassion and patience with yourself as you work on becoming more secure.

Clarifying Inner Conflict

Does a scrum of emotionally driven thoughts about yourself, your partner (or someone else), and a particular situation sometimes confuse and overwhelm you? You can gain greater clarity by developing a better perspective for seeing each of these thoughts and how they interact. This can lead to accepting these thoughts as coexisting—though sometimes conflicting—reactions within you.

Begin learning to gain this kind of clarity by identifying an example of a situation in which you have conflicting thoughts and feelings. How would you characterize the conflict? Here's an example: *I am crazy jealous. I'm always trying to get Billy to spend time with me, begging him not to go out with other friends. Even though Billy is consistently sweet and caring, I still worry that he's cheating.*

_____

_____

_____

Next use a chart to separate out your thoughts, emotions, and actions as they relate to yourself, the other person, and the situation. You can address the other person's reactions at the bottom. First, take a look at this completed chart, which is a continuation of the example just given:

Domain	Thoughts	Emotions	My Actions/Reactions
Self	I am a good partner.	Confident, happy	Happy when we are together Encourage Billy to spend time with other friends
	I'm not worthy of Billy.	Fear he will cheat; jealous	Try to get him to stay with me, not go out with friends Often accusing him of looking at other men
	I am such a loser, why would he want to be with me?	Angry with myself; unlovable, jealous, afraid he will leave me for someone else	All the same reactions to thinking I'm unworthy Cry when Billy is not around Try hard to please him
Other	Billy is trustworthy	Loving, happy	Affectionate
	Billy will get tired of me	Suspicious, jealous	Start fights with him Am clingy, too needy
Situation	Good relationship	In love	Enjoy time together
	Don't trust we'll stay together	Anxious, afraid, jealous	Always looking for how he's going to let me down or leave
	Both trying to make it work	Anxious, frustrated with myself	Make myself be okay with him going out without me
The other person's actions/reactions:	Billy is supportive and loving. He gets my insecurity, tells me all the good he sees in me, and is reassuring. But I can see he gets frustrated. And I think he's losing patience.		

Now it's your turn:

Domain	Thoughts	Emotions	My Actions/Reactions
Self			
Other			
Situation			
The other person's actions/reactions:			

Review your chart. What insights do you have? How might you resolve, live with, or escape the conflict? Example: *Even the good times are getting tense. If I don't get a grip, I will drive him away and make happen what I'm afraid is going to happen. I need to work on feeling more secure.*

_____

_____

_____

_____

_____

As with other exercises, you may find it helpful to explore this topic more in your journal or to complete this exercise with different situations. A blank template of this chart is available at https://drbecker-phelps. com/insecure-in-love-workbook or at http://www.newharbinger.com/52175.

Overcoming Your Obstacles to Happiness

Reflect on some positive memories—times when you enjoyed feeling safe (in a ventral vagal state). Did the positive feelings sometimes disappear as quickly as a raindrop on hot pavement, returning you to your insecure default mode of scanning for problems? Or did anxiety overshadow positive feelings? If you responded in either of these ways, you are not alone. Many people who were essentially trained to constantly scan for threats have not developed the ability to allow for, or hold on to, a sense of well-being. Sometimes they even register well-being as a sign of potential danger (that lowering their defenses to allow in the positive also opens them up to harm).

Describe five different experiences you have had with feeling positive or thinking you should have felt that way. They might range from full enjoyment to fleeting experiences to being more aware of accompanying anxiety.

1. _____

   _____

2. _____

   _____

3. _____

   _____

4. _____

   _____

5. _____

_____

Reflect on these experiences. What patterns do you see? Here are some examples of patterns you might experience:

- You feel comfortable with low arousal experiences, such as feeling calm or content.

- You feel uncomfortable with more energized emotions, such as feeling excited or playful.

- When situations are okay or even going well, you become anxious when you are alone, around people, just around men or just around women, or around people you don't know well.

_____

_____

_____

_____

_____

_____

_____

_____

Empathizing with your difficulty generating, maintaining, or returning to positive emotions can help you to compassionately remind yourself that you need to nurture and become more comfortable with them. (You may want to return to chapter 3 for exercises to help you with this.)

By learning to mentalize yourself and your partner, you are developing compassionate self-awareness and compassionate other-awareness. These skills are essential to your personal development and to nurturing healthy, secure relationships. However, your insecure attachment might still drive you to view yourself as unworthy and to criticize yourself. So, you may need to enhance your budding ability to mentalize by specifically building self-acceptance. You will work on this skill in the next chapter.

CHAPTER 9

Building Self-Acceptance

The proper foundation of a house insulates against problems even through natural disasters. Similarly, the proper foundation of a self remains intact even through personal emergencies. By contrast, when these foundations are weak or fragile, your home and self are at risk for coming apart from everyday "use" or being damaged by particularly stressful situations.

When it comes to your inner home, self-acceptance offers a strong foundation for a secure self. To be truly self-accepting, it is essential that you accept the following:

You are human. (Hopefully, this is not a stretch for you!)

Humans are flawed. (Said another way, no one is perfect.)

Once you accept these two statements, then the following is also true (for logic or math geeks, this follows the *modus ponens* rule and the transitive property, respectively): *You are flawed.*

I can almost feel you nodding with a silent *I knew it!* But this last statement must be understood within the context of the first two. In other words, weaknesses, making mistakes, and other difficult or painful experiences are part of being human. So, given that you are human, all of these experiences reveal your humanity—*not* that you are essentially flawed, deficient, unlovable, or don't belong to the human race. Even if that last statement doesn't feel right, you can hopefully acknowledge its fundamental truth.

This concept has been described by self-compassion researcher Kristin Neff as our *common humanity*. Reflect and write about it now, both as it relates to people in general, and as it relates specifically to you:

_____

_____

_____

_____

_____

Common humanity is the basis of self-acceptance and self-compassion. In this chapter, you will be working to nurture self-acceptance. (We will focus on self-compassion in chapter 10.)

The Truth Is You Are Lovable

All humans are fundamentally the same in more ways than we are different. One of those ways is that all of us are precious and lovable just for being born. This is true whether or not the adults around us can fully appreciate or honor that immutable fact. And it's true for you, too, whether or not you believe it. But do you believe it?

If not, consider this. Think about what defines human babies. They are pint-sized creatures who can't do a thing to care for themselves. They need to be fed. They pee. They poop. They need their diapers changed. They cry. (Some more than others, but they all do it.) And not a single one of them does anything to earn their keep. Other than the pleasure adults might get by caring for them, they are no help at all. Yet the vast majority of adults respond with a primal recognition that babies are inherently precious. It's unimaginable to judge any baby as unlovable, agreed?

As infants mature, become more mobile, and ultimately grow into big people, they continue to carry that spark of something special just for existing. There is no reason to think it would suddenly disappear at any particular point. But as they lose their baby cuteness—technically called *kindchenschema*—we can lose the awareness that they are precious. Loss of this awareness does not mean that it disappears, but we might find it harder to see. We continue to recognize it in those who are close to us, which is why you can have unconditional love for family or friends.

Now I'd like you to apply this unconditional love to yourself... Have I lost you? If so, you are in good company. Like so many other people, somewhere deep inside yourself, you might feel absolutely sure that you are inferior and are not lovable. However, rather than just accept this rejecting self-perception, ask yourself, *What makes me so different from everyone else? When I think about this, do I objectively believe I am all that different? Or is it just that my feelings of being unworthy and unlovable are so strong?* Remember that something can feel true without actually being true. As you respond to these questions, explore your emotional thoughts and feelings openly, in a respectful way that might cast some doubt on them but without trying to prove them wrong.

In doing this exercise, it is unlikely that you will be hit by lightning and suddenly exclaim, *I am lovable!* But if you begin to doubt the story you tell yourself about you being inferior, unworthy, or unlovable, then you have opened the possibility of relating to yourself in a more positive way.

Notice Your Strengths

Reflect on aspects of yourself that you feel good about—such as your values, traits, or abilities. Do you notice a bump in feeling good about you? Such self-affirmations can not only highlight secure feelings about yourself but can also make you more resilient to difficult situations and less likely to assume others will be critical of you.

Of course, before you can affirm your positives, you must identify them. For this exercise, you will be listing your traits, talents, and basic values that you feel good about. Consider this brainstorming, so don't leave anything out, no matter how small or superficial you think it might be.

List traits about yourself that you value, such as being funny, persistent, or creative.

_____

_____

List your talents, such as being good at painting, bargaining with car dealers, or helping others to feel good about themselves.

_____

_____

List the basic values that you live by, such as honesty, generosity, or having a good work ethic.

_____

_____

Review the lists you just made. How do you feel about yourself as you look at them? Do you feel even a little good about yourself? Or do you chastise yourself, delivering the message that it is not acceptable to feel good? If you do the latter, consider whether you might be kinder to a friend who allowed in positive feelings (without being boastful) about themselves.

_____

_____

_____

_____

_____

By completing your lists, you have created a pool of inner resources that you can use for self-affirmations, which you will be doing in the next few exercises. You might choose to develop a regular practice from just one or a combination of these exercises.

Affirming Your Positives

Referring back to the three lists in the "Notice Your Strengths" exercise, pick the three to five positive aspects of yourself that you value most. List them below. You will focus on just one in this workbook. If you wish, use your journal to complete the exercise for each of the others.

1. _____

2. _____

3. _____

4. _____

5. _____

Pick one positive aspect of yourself from your list to reflect on now: (Example: *I am funny.*) _____

Recall a specific experience that reflects this positive aspect of you: (Example: *I made Eric laugh when he was feeling down yesterday.*)

_____

_____

Now reflect on this experience. To help you do this, consider all of the domains of self-awareness (STEAM) that were part of the experience. By actually immersing yourself in what happened, rather than just remembering it from an objective perspective, you will be better able to mentalize—and fully appreciate—this positive aspect of yourself.

Sensations: (Example: *My body felt more relaxed when Eric seemed happier.*)

_____

_____

Thoughts: (Example: *Eric needed a good distraction.*)

_____

_____

Emotions: (Example: *Being able to make Eric laugh made me feel happy and useful.*)

_____

_____

Actions: (Example: *I was telling funny stories.*)

_____

_____

Mentalizing: (Example: *I was trying to make Eric laugh because he was feeling down and I wanted to help him. I feel good about myself for being a caring friend.*)

_____

_____

Consider using this exercise to create a daily practice. You might choose to reflect each day on a different positive aspect of yourself or on different examples of the same one. Be sure to use STEAM (either in writing or in just reflecting on each domain) to fully connect with affirming yourself.

Create a Personal Mantra

Create a personal mantra that you can repeat to yourself on a daily basis or whenever you feel you need a self-affirmation. Though your mantra should be simple, it can include a combination of different things you value about yourself. For example, your mantra could be: *I feed the soul of everyone in my family with my good cooking.* Or, it might be: *I have integrity and I'm great at making people laugh.*

Write your mantra: _____

_____

You can repeat this mantra daily by itself, or as part of a meditation practice. You might also use it to help bolster you when you are feeling distressed. If you are reciting it daily, choose a time when you will do it (e.g., before getting out of bed in the morning): _____

Journal Your Self-Affirmation

Choose one of your basic values that you identified in the "Notice Your Strengths" exercise.

_____

Why is this value important to you?

_____

_____

_____

Describe at least one time when you have lived this value, including what made it meaningful for you. Be sure to include observations about your emotions, such as how they helped motivate you to act on your value and what emotions you felt by living your value.

_____

_____

_____

_____

_____

If this exercise affirms a positive sense of yourself, try repeating it with other values that you live by.

Making Time for What Feels Good or Right

Do you make time for the things you enjoy or that are important to you? Part of self-acceptance is recognizing that you, your desires, and your happiness are important. This will naturally lead to sometimes focusing on what feels good or right to you rather than just on what you are accomplishing or on making others happy. This exercise will help you strengthen your sense of self-acceptance by including enjoyable and meaningful activities in your life. Because novelty and learning can be rewarding, think about trying new things. In addition, a change of scenery each day can add to your happiness, even if that means just going for a walk around your neighborhood or taking a different route to work.

In the chart below, do the following:

- Check off each activity that you have enjoyed or felt fulfillment from.

- Circle those checked-off activities that you would like to do more of in your life now.

- Star each activity that you have not done but would like to try.

☐ Watch TV shows/movies	☐ Daydream	☐ Groom (hair or nails salon)
☐ Watch sports on TV	☐ Go on vacation	☐ Plan a vacation
☐ Get a massage	☐ Go for a drive	☐ Ride a motorcycle
☐ Go to live comedy shows	☐ Spa day	☐ Do landscaping or garden
☐ Fix something	☐ Decorate your home	☐ Watch the sunrise or sunset
☐ Exercise	☐ Go out to dinner	☐ Do yoga, tai chi, etc.
☐ Dance	☐ Try new foods	☐ Cook
☐ Bake	☐ Meditate	☐ Pray
☐ Play a sport	☐ Picnic or barbecue	☐ Be active politically

☐ Swim	☐ Read a book or magazine	☐ Play games (e.g., cards)
☐ Fish	☐ Socialize	☐ Play an instrument
☐ Bicycle	☐ Learn a new skill	☐ Do creative writing
☐ Clean, organize	☐ Learn about a new topic	☐ Talk with friends, family
☐ Make crafts	☐ Listen to music	☐ Throw a party
☐ Shop	☐ Be affectionate	☐ Stroll in a town, city
☐ Do puzzles (e.g., jigsaw)	☐ Have a romantic date	☐ Attend live theater/concert
☐ Go to museums	☐ Have sex	☐ Collect things
☐ Go to aquariums	☐ Spend time at the beach	☐ Engage in a hobby
☐ Go for walks	☐ Hike or just be in nature	☐ Stargaze
☐ Hold or play with a pet	☐ Browse art galleries	☐ Go to an amusement park

Take a moment to appreciate the benefit you get (or have gotten) from the activities that you have checked off.

Of those that are circled or starred, choose one activity that you would like to begin adding to your life first. If you choose a starred activity, be sure to research what you need to know to begin:

_____

Clarify exactly what you would like to do. Be specific. Here are some examples. Ken wrote: I want to add a vegetable garden alongside my back deck. Cassie wrote: I want to jog for thirty minutes four times a week, on Mondays, Tuesdays, and Fridays at 7 a.m. before work and on Sunday mornings.

Your turn: _____

_____

_____

What steps do you need to take to make this happen? It is often helpful to be very specific, so you might want to do some research about how best to proceed, and then break your activity into steps. For this more in-depth approach, use your journal to write out the steps. For now, write in the steps that you know (which might include doing research to learn more). Ken wrote: I am going to look up what vegetables will grow best and how to create the best soil. After looking this up online, I'm going to visit Nan's Nursery to ask their advice and get started. Cassie wrote: I am really out of shape, so I'll start by walking for fifteen minutes. Then I'll add jogging and more walking or jogging as I'm able to. What are your steps?

_____

_____

_____

Prepare to start. Sometimes getting started is the hardest part of adding an activity to your life. If this is the case for you, what might help you get started? You might find it helpful to do the following:

- Use the self-affirmation exercises in this chapter to help strengthen your determination to attend to your own wants.

- Find ways to reward yourself for taking action.

- Set a date and specific time to start.

- Find a buddy to join you.

What can you do to help yourself get started?

_____

_____

_____

_____

Get started and attend to your experience. It's one thing to do something for yourself, and it's another to connect with the experience as you engage in it; and to feel positive as you reflect back on it. With this in mind, take time to actually do the activity while focusing on what you enjoy about it. Then return here.

Describe your experience, being sure to focus on the feel-good aspects of it.

_____

_____

_____

_____

Repeat this exercise when you feel it is time to add a new enjoyable or fulfilling activity into your life. You can heighten your positive feelings and sense of self-acceptance by journaling about these activities.

Express Your Authentic Self Creatively

Do you enjoy being creative? For example, maybe you enjoy dancing, drawing, or making videos on your phone. You probably like how being creative allows you to express your authentic self. Or, alternatively, maybe you steer clear of creative activities because they make you feel vulnerable, open to being judged. Either way, consider creating a self-affirmation collage as described here. It will encourage you to become more self-accepting by expressing yourself in a fun, unintimidating way. Follow these simple steps:

Assemble the materials. You will need glue, scissors, magazines to cut up, and any size piece of cardboard or poster board for the collage backing. You might also want to print images from your computer.

Clear a work space. Be sure to have sufficient space to lay out your materials.

Prepare your mind. Take some deep breaths and reflect on the self-affirmation exercises in this chapter, being open to whatever inner experiences come to you. This is the focus of your collage.

Collect images. Rather than looking for particular images in magazines, allow yourself to stumble upon ones that feel right. These might include pictures, designs, or words. But if you feel pulled to use images or words that are not in the magazines, you might find them online and then print them out. Also, feel free to draw or write out words to include in the collage.

Affix the images. You can glue down the images as you find them, or cut them all out and then arrange them. Remember that this is your personal collage, so do this in whatever way appeals to you.

Appreciate your work. Place your collage in a place where you will naturally see it in the course of your day. Practice seeing it in an open, nonjudgmental way. If you find yourself being critical, bring your mind back to perceiving rather than judging. Insights might unexpectedly dawn on you. If they do, take out your journal to record those thoughts, which you can read again later and reflect on.

The exercises in this chapter have hopefully helped you to open up to your true inner experiences in a nonjudgmental way, allowing you to develop greater self-acceptance. As a result, you may have a greater sense of feeling secure and more at home within yourself. However, developing self-acceptance can be really challenging, and you might become impatient or even angry with yourself at times. If you are struggling, try returning to the exercises in chapter 2 that help you develop a safe haven and a secure base, both of which will give you a sense of being supported and encouraged. You will also find help moving toward greater self-acceptance in the next chapter, which focuses on compassionate self-awareness.

CHAPTER 10

Nurturing Compassionate Self-Awareness

As you have been deepening your self-awareness and self-acceptance, what changes have you noticed in the way you relate to yourself? More specifically, have you noticed that you are at least sometimes not quite as quick to criticize yourself? Or that you are more likely to question your self-critical reactions? By opening to self-awareness and self-acceptance, you are creating a caring, welcoming, and warm home for *all* of your inner experiences. You are increasing empathy for yourself, which can then allow you to have self-compassion. To clarify, self-compassion means wanting to ease your own pain and to take good care of yourself. Altogether, you have been working to develop compassionate self-awareness.

However, you might still struggle with relating to yourself in positive, caring ways. The exercises in this chapter are designed to counter any lingering self-doubts and self-criticism with conscious efforts to develop greater self-compassion. This can help you feel more securely at home in yourself, especially during difficult situations.

To be more securely attached and have more secure relationships, it is essential that you can both take in caring from others and offer it to them. So, while the focus of this chapter is on developing compassionate self-awareness, the exercises also include notes about how you can strengthen your compassionate other-awareness.

Self-Compassion Is Not Self-Pity

Contrary to what many people think, having self-compassion is not the same as pitying yourself. As self-compassion researcher Kristin Neff points out, unlike self-compassion, self-pity fails to recognize that being human means making mistakes, having weaknesses, and sometimes being in emotional pain. So, while self-pity includes a sense that *There is something wrong with me*, self-compassion is based on the insight that *Although what I'm going through is difficult, I know that others have had similar struggles. It's part of being human.* While intellectually knowing that you are not alone may not stop your self-pity, this exercise uses your awareness to help you at least question it.

Explain a situation that you believe (or sense) shows that something is wrong with you and that causes you to sink into self-pity.

_____

_____

_____

As you think about the situation, briefly note your experience in these domains of STEAM:

Sensations: _____

Thoughts: _____

Emotions: _____

Actions: _____

Imagine that someone else (maybe your partner or a good friend) is facing the same situation and the same emotional dilemma. How do you feel toward this person? If you do not initially feel compassion, it may help to spend more time trying to truly understand their struggle.

_____

_____

_____

_____

Next, think about this: Do you feel differently toward them than you feel toward yourself? Is your focus more on wanting to alleviate their pain or wishing they were not in pain, rather than on judging them for their situation? If so, you are empathizing with their human reaction and experiencing compassion rather than feeling pity or being judgmental. Now try to feel that compassion for yourself.

What is your reaction to this thought experiment? Are you able to have self-compassion, even for a moment? If not, does it at least cast some doubt on your self-judgment and self-pity?

_____

_____

_____

_____

_____

_____

_____

Remember, the purpose of this exercise is not necessarily to stop your self-criticism and self-pity, though it would be good if this happened. Instead, the more modest goal is to help you question your sense of being essentially flawed and to open up to self-compassion.

Having Self-Compassion Is Not Being Self-Centered

Just as you wouldn't want a surgeon operating on you if they had not slept or eaten for twenty-four hours, those who depend on you need—and deserve—you at your best. You short-change yourself _and_ others when you forego sleep, healthy eating, proper exercise, and other facets of prudent self-care. The idea here is that caring about yourself, which includes having self-compassion, is important _in addition to_—not instead of—caring about others. As Christopher Germer expressed so well in his book _The Mindful Path to Self-Compassion_: "In a room full of people, it makes sense to help the person who's suffering the most, the one we know best, the one we're most capable of helping. Sometimes that person is you..." (2009, 89).

Think about something you do (or want to do) that causes you to struggle with feeling self-centered. For instance, you might want to enjoy a weekend away with friends but feel guilty at the thought of leaving your spouse alone. Forgetting other people for the moment, what are the immediate and long-term benefits of doing this for you? Is it understandable that you would want those benefits?

_____

_____

_____

_____

What are the immediate and long-term effects on others?

_____

_____

_____

Finally, for the moment, put aside your struggles with feeling self-centered, as you reflect on this situation. Consider how fulfilling (or even partially fulfilling) it would be to meet your wants or desires. Then consider the negative effects that doing this may have on others. Be sure to factor in the relative importance (or lack of importance) of those relationships in your life.

_____

_____

_____

_____

_____

Pay attention to how self-compassion does not exclude considering the needs of others, too.

Self-Compassion Does Not Get You "Off the Hook"

Responding to an action you regret with self-compassion is *not* the same as letting yourself off the hook (Neff 2011). While the sting of every self-critical thought may work as a self-punishment, much like the thwack of being hit by a stick, it also reinforces your sense of unworthiness. Instead, when you recognize your mistake with self-compassion, a desire for your own well-being can be a "carrot" to improve. It's a much more effective approach to helping you be a better you. To gain a better understanding of how this works, complete this exercise:

Write down a common harsh criticism you often make of yourself.

_____

_____

Bring to mind either your child (at a young age if they are an adult now), a child you have known, or one you have simply observed. You might even drive to a local park to watch children play. Whichever option you choose, allow yourself to feel positive toward them. Now imagine them having a struggle similar to what you criticize yourself for. Imagine you criticizing them the way you criticize yourself. How do you think they would feel? What might they do?

_____

_____

_____

_____

Mentalize the child—understanding and connecting with their thoughts and emotions related to their weakness or struggles. Empathize with the pain it causes them, and be open to feeling compassion, a sincere desire for them not to hurt. Imagine communicating your understanding, caring, support, and encouragement. How do you think they would feel? How would they react? Notice how your compassion may be helping them feel positive about themselves and motivated to change.

_____

_____

_____

_____

_____

_____

Finally, think again about your self-criticism or insecurity. But this time, try to respond to yourself as you responded to that child. Using compassionate self-awareness, write down your responses.

_____

_____

_____

_____

_____

_____

Everyone Deserves Self-Compassion

Do you question whether you have inherent value, doubting that you deserve self-compassion? If so, hopefully the exercises in this chapter are helping you discover your worthiness and opening you to self-compassion. However, if you become frustrated in completing these exercises, you may need to gain a greater understanding and appreciation of how you were taught to feel unworthy. This is the work of mentalizing yourself, which is detailed in chapter 8. Return there to repeat the exercises, if appropriate.

If you still feel stuck after trying to complete the exercises in this chapter and in chapter 8, consider finding a therapist. Attachment theory tells us that we originally learn to identify with how lovable and worthy (or unlovable and unworthy) we are through the eyes of our caregivers. As adults, we sometimes need professional help to change our fundamental relationship with ourselves to one that is more appreciative and caring.

What's Your Level of Self-Compassion?

Self-compassion researcher Kristin Neff (2011) explains that self-compassion involves three elements: self-kindness, common humanity, and mindfulness. *Self-kindness* is simply treating yourself with kindness, with the intention of trying to help yourself be a healthy, happy person. *Common humanity* is the sense that all people share common experiences, including pain and suffering, weaknesses, and making mistakes. *Mindfulness* is being nonjudgmentally aware of, and accepting of, the current moment.

This exercise is a self-assessment for each of these elements of self-compassion. On a scale of 1 to 5, in which 1 means not at all and 5 means completely, rate how well you identify with the following statements. For each element of self-compassion, calculate a final score by adding the ratings and dividing the total by the number of statements.

Self-Kindness

_____ You are accepting and gentle with yourself in response to your imperfections or inadequacies.

_____ You are accepting and gentle with yourself when you make mistakes.

_____ You are caring and nurture yourself when you are hurting or emotionally upset.

_____ You want to treat yourself well, so you can be happy in the long term.

_____ Total

Final score: Total ÷ 4 = _____

Common Humanity

_____ You believe others have weaknesses, imperfections, or inadequacies just like you do.

_____ You can see your struggles as part of being human, that you are not alone in them.

_____ When upset, you can remember that other people sometimes have similar struggles and feelings.

_____ Remembering that other people sometimes have similar struggles and feelings helps you feel less alone.

_____ Total

Final score: Total ÷ 4 = _____

Mindfulness

_____   You can accept your thoughts and feelings without judging them, even when you're upset.

_____   You can accept your thoughts and feelings without denying, suppressing, or exaggerating them.

_____   You can experience your emotions without becoming overly identified with them and losing perspective.

_____   When upset or during challenging times, you try to maintain a healthy perspective.

_____   Total

Final score: Total ÷ 4 = _____

The higher your score for any area (the highest score being 5), the stronger you are in it. What strengths, weaknesses, or other patterns do you see?

_____

_____

_____

_____

_____

Practice Absorbing Compassion from Loved Ones

If you have difficulty taking in compassion from loved ones, you may find that learning to do this can help you nurture self-compassion. To develop this ability, think of a situation in which you were suffering and your partner or another loved one showed you compassion. They were clearly empathizing with you and wanting good things for you. Describe the situation and the person's response.

_____

_____

_____

_____

If you feel compelled to argue with their perspective, acknowledge this, but then focus on their positive thoughts and caring feelings toward you. Note any physical or emotional reactions. Do you feel at all comforted?

_____

_____

_____

_____

You may need to do this many times before you can hold a positive experience without reverting to your insecurity. You might also journal about other experiences to practice absorbing compassion shown to you.

Practice Self-Compassion

Reflect on the last exercise, connecting with the compassion offered by your loved one. Now replay the situation in your mind, maintaining that same compassionate perspective toward yourself. If you slip back into self-criticism, simply try again.

Describe your experience in doing this. Did you feel any self-compassion? Did you have to repeatedly bring yourself back to a self-compassionate perspective? If you found this difficult, what thoughts or emotions interfered with it? To what degree can you put them aside as you refocus on offering yourself compassion?

_____

_____

_____

_____

_____

_____

_____

Are you still unable to offer yourself compassion? That's okay. This can be really hard to do. You might find it helpful to get out your journal and write about the domains of STEAM for this situation. You can also use the worksheet "Gain Self-Awareness Through STEAM," which is available online at https://drbecker-phelps.com/insecure-in-love-workbook or at http://www.newharbinger.com/52175. When you complete the mentalizing domain, this is your opportunity to encourage self-compassion; to reflect on the other domains of STEAM so that you can truly empathize with and feel caring toward your experience.

As you work to nurture self-compassion, also try to be compassionate to your partner and other loved ones. By doing this, you will nurture healthy relationships.

Attain Compassionate Self-Awareness with "Of Course, I…"

When you are truly able to gain compassionate self-awareness, you will see your struggles with understanding and an appreciation for your experience. You will have a sense of *Of course, I am struggling like this.*

To help you attain this perspective, describe a specific incident when you struggled with feeling insecure in your current relationship.

_____

_____

_____

Briefly note your experience in these domains of STEAM:

Sensations: _____

Thoughts: _____

Emotions: _____

Actions: _____

Mentalize yourself. While connecting with your awareness in all of these domains, reflect deeply on your experience, so that you can—to the best that you are able—more fully appreciate, empathize with, and have compassion for your experience. Make some notes about this:

_____

_____

_____

_____

_____

Heighten your self-compassion. Reflect on past experiences that laid the foundation for your current reactions. This might mean recalling memories as far back as childhood or more recent memories, such as from your last intimate relationship. Explain this insight here and then take the time to really let it settle into you. (If you are not aware of how your past might be playing into your present experience, return to the chapter 8 exercise "What's in Your Luggage?")

_____

_____

_____

_____

_____

_____

_____

Respond with "Of course, I… Reflect on what you've completed in this exercise until your empathic understanding seems to click. At that point, it will seem natural to say to yourself, *Of course, I responded this way given my experience.* Write your "Of course, I…" statement here, making sure to explain it in detail.

_____

_____

_____

_____

_____

Practice repeating this exercise in your journal. The more you are able to attain and maintain this kind of insight, the more you will feel greater security in yourself. You will also be able to face problems in relationships from a more self-assured stance, and with an ability to be more open and vulnerable, when appropriate. Finally, you might find that you are better able to mentalize your partner so that you can have empathy and compassion for them, and thus work through differences in a more constructive and caring way.

Loving-Kindness Meditation

Loving-kindness meditations encourage you to experience a sense of personal worth and to increase feelings of social connection. With practice, you will be able to "feel the love."

Sit down and settle into a comfortable position. Close or lower your eyes.

Bring your awareness to your breath. Follow the flow of your inhale and exhale for several breaths.

Bring your awareness to the heart area of your chest and repeat the following:

May I feel safe.

May I feel healthy.

May I feel peaceful and happy.

May I feel loved.

Recite each of these phrases slowly—silently or aloud—allowing them to wash over you in a way that you can truly absorb. Remember, this is a wish, not a command.

After you are able to connect with this meditation, you might want to focus on others: family, friends, acquaintances, or even people you've never met (*May they feel safe*). The more you practice this, the stronger your sense of compassion will grow.

If you struggle with offering these loving wishes to yourself, try offering them first to someone you already feel loving toward. Then try repeating the meditation with a focus on you. If this proves too difficult, recognize and appreciate your efforts just the same. With practice, you will improve your ability to wish yourself loving-kindness.

Complete this meditation by returning awareness to your breath. Allow time to sit with the peaceful, positive feelings that accompanied the wishes of loving-kindness.

Consider making the loving-kindness meditation a daily practice. Journaling about your experience might help you more fully appreciate its effect upon you and thus encourage you to repeat it.

Imagine a Compassionately Self-Aware You

You can develop self-compassion by imagining what you might be like as a more self-compassionate person and then responding to yourself from this perspective. Give it a try. You can access a recording of this exercise online at https://drbecker-phelps.com/insecure-in-love-workbook or at http://www.newharbinger.com /52175.

Think about times when you've been compassionate to yourself or others. What traits come to mind, including those that have developed while working on the exercises in this book? Describe them here.

_____

_____

_____

_____

List all the traits of a compassionate person that you can think of. You may find it helpful to think about someone in your life (past or present), a religious or historical figure (for example, Mother Theresa, Mahatma Gandhi, Martin Luther King, Jr.), or a fictional character from a novel or film.

_____

_____

_____

_____

Imagine your future self as embodying self-compassion. What would this self look like? What would you be wearing? How would you hold yourself? What traits would you have?

_____

_____

_____

_____

_____

_____

_____

_____

Now sit comfortably, perhaps with your eyes closed, and think of the word "insecurity." Allow memories related to this word to come to you and then pick one memory. To help you really re-experience the memory, attend to your sensations, thoughts, and emotions.

Imagine your future compassionate self approaching you. This compassionately self-aware version of you knows everything you have experienced in the world and within yourself. You tell this future self all about your struggles and pain. As they listen, they somehow communicate compassion, perhaps in words, a look, or a gesture. Allow yourself to absorb their caring. If you are hesitant to do this or feel defensive, share your reaction with your compassionate self. They will again respond with understanding, warmth, and acceptance. Continue the dialogue until you can take in at least some of the caring.

When you feel ready, thank your future self and then return your attention to the room you are sitting in. Describe you experience here.

_____

_____

_____

_____

_____

_____

_____

This is an experience you can return to anytime to help increase your inner calm and to strengthen your compassionate self-awareness. Note: If you find it too difficult to imagine a future compassionate self, try this exercise with one of the figures you thought of when you reflected on the elements of compassion. After successfully doing this exercise with that figure, try again with a compassionately self-aware future self.

Help Your Future Self

Everyone has ups and downs. Imagine how powerful it would be for the "up" version of you to encourage you when you are feeling down. No one else could possibly understand you better, and so no one else's words could possibly be more motivating. While you can't time travel, you can write a compassionate letter to your future self. When you are emotionally strong, do the following:

Reflect on situations when you've felt distressed. Observe your sensations, thoughts, and emotions at those times. As you do, nurture a sense of empathy and compassion for your distressed self. Also, consider what has helped you feel better, such as listening to music, going for a walk, or calling a friend.

Address a letter to your future distressed self, focusing on compassion for them. You might do the following:

Tell them that they have value and that you care about them.

Tell them that they will feel better. Explain that you have experience with rebounding emotionally.

Offer concrete advice that has sometimes worked for you in the past.

Make notes here about what you would like to say in your letter, which you can write on a fresh sheet of paper (or type and print out).

_____

_____

_____

_____

_____

_____

_____

_____

_____

After you have completed the letter, be sure to put it in an accessible place.

Now that you have worked on developing compassionate self-awareness, it is time to put that new skill to work in nurturing a healthy relationship.

CHAPTER 11

Finding a Good Match

Are you looking for the perfect partner? If so, your best dating advice might actually come from an old, yet timeless, source of wisdom: Voltaire, the French Enlightenment writer stated, "Perfect is the enemy of the good." In the dating world, this means that you may never find a great (or even a good) match if you are focused solely on finding a perfect partner. It's just too high a bar for anyone.

Also, as you think about the partner you would like to meet, seriously consider these questions: Can you imagine openheartedly accepting that you have found a wonderful partner who is deeply thankful to have met you? Or would meeting such a person likely grip you with anxiety and confusion about why they would want to be with you? If it's the latter, then your imagined relationship may be doomed before it starts.

In your quest for a partner, you may find it helpful to practice thinking about what would make *you* happy. Allow for the possibility that a romantic partner can see the real you *and* love that person, even if it is hard to believe right now. Does this seem as likely as you touching the moon with your feet firmly planted on earth? If so, then try to build greater self-acceptance by returning to the exercises in chapter 9.

The truth is that the only way you can fully enjoy a healthy, secure relationship is if you find someone whose presence in your life supports you feeling good about being your authentic self. The exercises in this chapter are designed to help you find someone who meets that description and who can work collaboratively with you to nurture the relationship you want.

What Are You Looking for in a Partner?

Consider what you want in a partner as well as how important each trait is to you. *Be honest.* Describing what you think you "should" want will only interfere with finding what will ultimately make you happy.

What physical traits and aspects of appearance would you like your partner to have? How important are these things?

_____

_____

_____

_____

What personality traits are you looking for in a partner? How important are these things?

_____

_____

_____

_____

What aspects of a partner's occupation are important to you?

_____

_____

_____

_____

What are you looking for in terms of your partner's lifestyle, interests, life priorities (including religion), and leisure activities?

_____

_____

_____

_____

What are you looking for in terms of parenting including whether you want to be a parent, beliefs about each person's parenting roles, and styles of parenting?

_____

_____

_____

_____

_____

Is there anything else you are looking for?

_____

_____

_____

_____

_____

Detailed responses can give you a good idea of what you are looking for. However, too many must-haves can make finding a suitable partner impossible. In fact, if you think you are being too particular, consider whether this is your attempt to protect yourself by making it just as likely to find a romantic match as to bump into a leprechaun (whose help you could surely use!). Be open to the possibility that what actually attracts you may not be what you expect.

Developing a Healthy Pattern of Self-Disclosure

When you feel anxious about meeting or spending time with a potential partner, your body is attuned to the possible threat of rejection. In response, do you tend to protect yourself by sharing very little? Do you feel a deep desire to be known and reassured, leading to a tidal wave of self-disclosure? Or, do you tend to protect yourself in a different way? If your self-protective mechanism undermines the natural process of getting to know someone who might be a good fit for you, then this exercise may help you develop a healthier pattern of self-disclosure:

Identify your unhealthy patterns as a first step toward interrupting them. Ask yourself, _What do I tend to do? What are my motivations for disclosing or not disclosing?_

_____

_____

_____

_____

_____

_____

_____

Develop a plan for what to disclose on your first dates. While you might be more or less comfortable sharing with different people, it can help to decide ahead of time any limits to what you think is wise to disclose. Ask yourself, *What do I feel comfortable sharing? What do I feel more comfortable waiting to share? What are topics that I believe I absolutely should not share yet, even if I have a desire to talk about them in the moment?*

_____

_____

_____

_____

_____

_____

_____

_____

Connect with a supportive person before your dates. You might discuss the upcoming date or even just chat about a totally different topic. Talking with a supportive friend who values you can bolster a positive sense of yourself and lessen the intensity of your fear of being judged or rejected. This can help you to relax your tendency to hyperfocus on protecting yourself, enabling you to turn your attention to getting to know your date. A friend's support can also help you feel okay about yourself if a date does not go well. With all of this in mind, who are the best people to reach out to?

_____

During your date, reflect on the other person's responsiveness. You might want to journal about this later, perhaps asking yourself: *Did their responses show that they were really listening to and showing an interest in me? Were they sharing enough about themselves to give me a glimpse into who they are? What did I like about them? What did I not like about them? Is there enough about them that I would want to continue getting to know?*

Consider whether the self-disclosures were balanced. Relationships are developed by each person sharing increasingly more personal information as the connection deepens. Of course, any particular interaction might include one person sharing more, but relationships work best when there is balanced sharing overall. With this in mind, after a date, you might want to answer these questions in your journal: *How balanced were self-disclosures during our date? How do I feel about this? If I still want to go on another date with them, is there more that I would like to share or would like them to share?*

Getting to know each other is an unfolding process. By attending to how you and your date each share, you can facilitate a healthy process of opening up.

Is Your Date Partner Material?

You will ultimately need to make a judgment about whether the person you are dating is right for you. You will likely be happiest with someone who is a safe haven (who comforts you during emotionally difficult times) and a secure base (who encourages you to be your best self).

Listed below are categories of basic traits of such a person. Under each category, check off all the descriptions that apply to the person you are dating or have met even once.

Securely Attached and Mature

☐ Comfortable with themselves

☐ Can be emotionally close/intimate

☐ Pursues their own interests

☐ Supports you in pursuing your interests

☐ Introspective and personally insightful

☐ Acknowledges and accepts their limitations

☐ Nondefensively admits their mistakes

☐ Maintains a positive sense of themselves

☐ Is forgiving of your mistakes and weaknesses

An Effective Communicator

☐ Good listener

☐ Shares appropriately about themselves (opening up about their personal experiences without dominating the conversation or making conversations all about them)

☐ Talks through tense conversations or disagreements in a constructive way

Appreciates You

☐ Respectful of you

☐ Values you

☐ Shows a continuing interest in learning about you

☐ Supports and encourages you to explore your personal interests

A Good Fit

☐ Enjoy some shared interests

☐ Enjoy spending time together

☐ Respect each other's values

☐ Share values that affect daily life

Ready for a Committed Relationship

☐ Makes your relationship a priority by devoting time and attention to it

☐ Makes emotional closeness a priority

☐ Views physical affection, including sex, as important to the relationship

☐ Believes that you are both responsible for comforting and caring for each other as well yourselves

As you reflect on the descriptions you checked, as well as those you did not, keep in mind that a partner who is good for you does not need to match up with everything on this list. It's more important to think about how their profile fits with your preferences and emotional needs. What are your thoughts about this?

_____

_____

_____

_____

_____

_____

Are there any red flags that you think you should pay attention to, even if they are not a deal-breaker right now?

_____

_____

_____

_____

Imagining a Healthier Relationship

To enjoy a healthy relationship, you must nurture security between you and your partner. The questions in this exercise will help you think through your relationship, making it more likely that you will act in ways to nurture it.

What do you think it would feel like to be in a relationship with a loving, supportive partner? While it would undoubtedly bring lots of good to your life, also be sure to consider any ways in which it might be uncomfortable or difficult for you.

_____

_____

_____

_____

_____

_____

As your attachment anxiety lessens with the inner work you are doing (but does not necessarily disappear), how will your emotions and actions in this healthy relationship be different from the past?

_____

_____

_____

_____

What healthy coping skills might you use to manage the anxiety that still exists?

_____

_____

_____

_____

How might your reactions (emotional and behavioral) affect your partner? More specifically, how might your partner respond to your current level of attachment anxiety? And how do you think this might be different from the ways previous partners have reacted to you?

_____

_____

_____

_____

_____

What signs will show you that your relationship is healthy or at least healthier than past ones? Consider your and your partner's reactions as well as patterns in your interactions. You might include examples of how quickly or slowly your relationship deepens: maintaining good communication, negotiating conflicts while being respectful, making each other a priority, and showing or having trust. You might also note signs that you are likely to see at different points in time, such as early on or late in your relationship.

_____

_____

_____

_____

_____

_____

_____

_____

_____

Reread your answers. Try to imagine the relationship that you are describing. As you see it more clearly, you might add or change what you've written. Once you think and feel that it is a good description of the relationship you want, read it again slowly, letting yourself really connect with it. You might even return to it again and again as you date, or to just think about your dream relationship. Let it guide you. Journal about how a new relationship compares to what you've written. Reflect on your personal growth and your current opportunity to create a healthier relationship.

Is Your Dud Date Worth Another Try?

Think about a time when you went on a date with someone who was attractive and interesting, but they didn't make your heart race or cause that little flip in your belly. Your assessment: no attraction and time to move on. *Let's pause here and reassess.*

Part of what releases butterflies inside a securely attached person who is dating is the excitement about meeting someone they like as well as the fear that the other person might not return their interest. When they click with someone who continues to accept them fully in the early stages of their relationship, they still feel excited, but their fears of rejection subside.

As a person who is insecurely attached, you expect that you will forever need to *earn* acceptance or else will be rejected or abandoned. As a result, you see anxiety as an inherent part of love. So, in the upside-down world of insecure attachment, if you click so well with someone that you feel truly accepted, you interpret the lack of anxiety as a lack of romantic interest. You label the date a dud.

By learning to recognize this dynamic, you can work to change it. Try evaluating the potential of a previous "dud date" in a different way. For example, consider these questions: Did your conversation flow? Were there things about the person that you liked? Did you share interests? Are they someone you could possibly see as physically attractive even if you were not feeling it in the moment?

_____

_____

_____

_____

_____

Reconsidering the date with the advantage of hindsight, do you think that the real problem may have been that they were actually a comforting presence…and that you were not afraid of being rejected? Do you think it would have been a good idea to give that person another chance?

_____

_____

_____

_____

Whatever your thoughts are about the example you chose, use this exercise as an opportunity to learn to reassess future dud dates as potential great matches.

Put an End to Your Pursuit-Withdrawal Dance

Think about whether you can relate to Katie's story: She met Justin through friends about two years ago. Sparks flew from the moment their eyes met. But after about a month, Justin began canceling plans so he could meet up with his buddies. Katie would text nonstop, looking for assurance that he wasn't cheating or planning to break up. He would reassure her, calming her fears. But then, as they got closer, he would withdraw again, by texting others a lot while they were together, sometimes failing to respond to her texts, not making plans to get together…and even forgetting about their dates! Each time, she would get upset— expressing increasingly more hurt and anger—until he calmed and comforted her again. Finally, he said he was done, and he stopped returning her calls and texts.

This pursuit-withdrawal dynamic is one of the most common patterns in troubled relationships. If you believe it is a pattern in your current or past relationships, use the following checklist to clarify how it plays out, or has played out, for you. This exercise assumes that you are the anxiously attached partner. Check off every statement that matches what you have experienced as well as what you think your partner (or previous partner) has experienced:

☐ *There is a pattern of my partner repeatedly getting closer and then more distant.*

☐ *Even though I'm in a relationship, I often feel lonely.*

☐ *I wish my partner was more—or more consistently—affectionate.*

☐ *I often try desperately to get back to the closeness we used to feel.*

☐ *I don't feel like a priority. It's like my partner is phoning it in.*

☐ *I wish my partner would spend more time with me.*

☐ *I wish my partner would give me more reassurance that I'm okay and that they really want me.*

☐ *My partner is tired of trying to reassure me.*

☐ *My partner often just tries to do what I want, so I won't get angry.*

☐ *My partner thinks I'm too needy and emotionally sensitive.*

☐ *My partner repeatedly becomes emotionally distant or is physically not around.*

☐ *I think a lot about what I can do to make my partner want to be closer to me.*

☐ *I often desperately try to regain a sense of closeness that seems beyond my reach.*

☐ *Even though I show an interest in my partner's life, they don't show much interest in mine.*

☐ *I'm often worried about being rejected or abandoned by my partner—yet again.*

☐ *I love when we are close, but then my partner becomes distant.*

Reflect on the statements you have checked off. Do you see the pursuit-withdrawal pattern in your relationship? Or do you notice other patterns? For example, maybe you are very insecure, but you effectively refrain from "pursuing" your partner, or your partner does not withdraw.

_____

_____

_____

_____

_____

_____

_____

_____

If you realize that you are caught in a pursuit-withdrawal pattern, then decide whether you believe it is best to work on the relationship or end it. If your attempts to change the pattern don't work, then you might try couples therapy. If you decide it's time to move on, use your developing compassionate self-awareness to help you move forward with ending the relationship.

Practice Nurturing Secure Relationships

You can prepare yourself for secure romantic relationships by nurturing secure friendships. Though similar patterns of insecurity may appear in friendships, they tend to be less intense than in romantic relationships. This makes it easier to work on improving those relationships and recognizing when it is best to leave them behind. Also, by nurturing many secure connections, the loss of any one of them (including a romantic one) will be less upsetting because you will still have other relationships to rely on.

You may want to review the chapter 2 exercises that encourage you to nurture friendships in which you and your friends are safe havens and secure bases for each other. Thinking about these relationships can help you prepare for dating by affirming your inherent value and lovability and by showing you how you already have the capacity to nurture secure connections.

To help strengthen your sense of being able to have secure relationships, name two or three friends with whom you have a secure connection, and write down what they value in you and what you value in them.

Friend 1: _____

What they value in me: _____

_____

What I value in them: _____

_____

Friend 2: _____

What they value in me: _____

_____

What I value in them: _____

_____

Friend 3: _____

What they value in me: _____

_____

What I value in them: _____

_____

Now, turn your attention back to your desire for a partner who makes you happy. When you meet someone who you think has the potential for being that person, use your friendships to remind you of what you deserve in relationships and of what you have to offer.

Calming Through Co-Regulation

Has your partner ever helped you calm down when you were upset? Have you ever lifted your partner's spirits when they were sad? If so, you were engaged in *co-regulation*. That is, you were helping each other manage, or regulate, your emotions. Rather than feeling alone in the world, you both felt connected and supported in your emotional struggles.

Talk with your partner about how you can consciously help each other. Understanding that different situations call for different responses, consider the following ways that you can be there for each other. In the first column of boxes, check off what your partner can do to comfort you when you are upset. The second column of boxes is for your partner to indicate what you can do to help them.

You	Partner	
		Offer a hug
		Hold hands
		Massage (scalp, shoulders, feet, hands)
		Go for a walk together
		Do breathing with you (see "Using Your Breath to Relax" in chapter 3)
		Cuddle as you watch a movie
		Active listening
		Offer comforting words (*It will be okay; I love you*). What words would you choose? _____
		Go to an event (such as live music). What are your preferences? _____

Write any other thoughts you have about how your partner can help you. For example, they might give you space when you are stomping around angrily and then offer to listen once you have calmed down a bit.

_____

_____

_____

_____

Similarly, write any other thoughts your partner has about how you can help them.

_____

_____

_____

_____

Check in occasionally to stay current on how you can help each other.

Reevaluating Your Relationship

The exercises you've been working on in this chapter are designed to nurture strong relationships. However, not every relationship is meant to last. If you are unsure about wanting to remain in a relationship that you are in, then it is time to carefully assess how well it is meeting your needs.

Using the three basic building blocks of secure attachment, this exercise will help you make a decision. Rate how well each of the following statements describes your partner by using a scale of 1 to 5, in which 1 means not at all and 5 means very well:

Safe Haven

_____   Communicates that they really hear and understand you

_____   Expresses a desire to be there for you when you struggle

_____   Responds to your distress with caring, reassurance, and support

_____   Just being in their presence feels comforting

Secure Base

_____   Shows an interest in what's important to you

_____   Wants you to be the best version of yourself

_____   Encourages you to explore your interests

_____   Is consistent in their support and encouragement

_____   Is supportive even when you differ in opinions or interests

Proximity (Emotionally Close and Available)

_____   Their presence, or your awareness of them, is comforting.

_____   Their presence, or your awareness of them, feels encouraging for you to explore yourself and the world.

Using these ratings, think about how well your partner meets your needs in these areas. You might also want to revisit "Is Your Date Partner Material?" in chapter 11. In addition, consider these questions: In what ways are you happy with your partner and your relationship? In what ways do your partner and your relationship fall short? In response to the problem areas that you identify, do you want to let things slide, work on the issues, or end the relationship? In addition to writing your thoughts here, you might find it helpful to talk with your partner or discuss this with a friend or a therapist.

_____

_____

_____

_____

_____

_____

_____

How to Let Go and Move On

If you are going through a breakup—whether it was you or your partner who decided to end your relationship—the loss can be difficult. So, consider these recommendations.

Offer yourself compassion. Even if your relationship had become a disaster, it was still important to you, and so you may need to mourn its loss. If this pain prompts your insecurity to resurface, remind yourself that the relationship ending does not mean there is something wrong with you. Still, it hurts. To soothe the pain, you may find it helpful to return to the compassionate self-awareness exercises in chapter 10.

Reach out to your support system. Name supportive people who can help you through this dark time.

_____

Remind yourself of your value and strengths. Help yourself move forward by connecting with what makes you feel good about you. Try returning to the exercises in chapter 9 to build greater self-acceptance.

Choose healthy ways of coping. You know what these are, but if you need guidance, use the exercises in "How to Soothe Your Nervous System" in chapter 3.

Be prepared for the urge to reunite. Think twice—maybe even thrice—before you act on impulses to reach out to your partner. Remind yourself why the relationship ended, perhaps even writing down the reasons. Talk it over with a supportive friend. If you do decide to return, be clear about your reasons and what you hope will be different this time.

Part of healing from a breakup is learning from that relationship experience. What went well? What was a problem? To help you let go and move on to a more secure relationship, write out your thoughts about this.

_____

_____

_____

_____

_____

_____

_____

Entering Your Future with a More Secure Self

Whether you are currently single, ending a relationship, or continuing to nurture one, you are on the journey of your lifetime. Think back to when you first started this workbook. Compare that person to who you are now. What progress have you made in feeling more at home within yourself? In what ways have you moved closer to being able to find or maintain an emotional home with a partner?

_____

_____

_____

_____

_____

_____

_____

Postscript

Simply by investing your time and energy in this workbook, you have undoubtedly made progress in becoming more secure in yourself and in being able to do so in a relationship—in finding your way home. The last exercise in chapter 11 was designed to help you recognize this growth. So, if you have not already completed it, do that now. (I mean *right now*. Then return here.)

As with any large undertaking, periodically reviewing it can help consolidate the gains you have made and strengthen weak areas. So, look back through the exercises you completed and through your journaling. As you do, be open to focusing on anything you would benefit from exploring more. Continue to use the domains of STEAM to develop your self-awareness and nurture empathy and compassion for your struggles. This compassionate self-awareness will naturally lead you to offer yourself greater support and encouragement. It will also help you be more open to others who are truly emotionally available.

Importantly, developing compassionate self-awareness will help you develop stronger compassionate other-awareness. This is crucial, because self-focus for its own sake can lead you down a path of self-preoccupation, a path that leads away from healthy connection with others and the world. Instead, with compassionate self- and other-awareness, you can build a strong, secure connection with yourself and a partner (as well as with family, friends, your community, nature, and maybe even a higher power, whatever that means to you).

With all your efforts to alleviate your relationship anxiety, never lose sight of how being secure in love starts with compassionate self-awareness. It will nurture your ability to finally feel more peacefully at home within yourself and ready to feel securely at home with a partner.

References

Ainsworth, Mary D. S., Mary C. Blehar, Everett Waters, and Sally N. Wall. 1978. *Patterns of Attachment: A Psychological Study of the Strange Situation*. Hillsdale, NJ: Lawrence Erlbaum.

Bartholomew, Kim, and Leonard M. Horowitz. 1991. "Attachment Styles Among Young Adults: A Test of a Four-Category Model." *Journal of Personality and Social Psychology* 61(2): 226–44.

Becker-Phelps, Leslie. 2014. *Insecure in Love: How Anxious Attachment Can Make You Feel Jealous, Needy, and Worried and What You Can Do About It*. Oakland, CA: New Harbinger Publications.

———. 2019. *Bouncing Back from Rejection: Build the Resilience You Need to Get Back Up When Life Knocks You Down*. Oakland, CA: New Harbinger Publications.

Bowlby, John. 1969. *Attachment and Loss*. Vol. 1, *Attachment*. New York: Basic Books.

Bratman, Gregory N., Christopher B. Anderson, Marc G. Berman, Bobby Cochran, Sjerp de Vries, Jon Flanders, Carl Folke, et al. 2019. "Nature and Mental Health: An Ecosystem Service Perspective." *Science Advances* 5(7): eaax0903. https://doi.org/10.1126/sciadv.aax0903.

Brennan, Kelly A., Catherine L. Clark, and Phillip R. Shaver. 1998. "Self-Report Measurement of Adult Romantic Attachment: An Integrative Overview." In *Attachment Theory and Close Relationships*, edited by Jeffry A. Simpson and W. Steven Rholes. New York: Guilford Press.

Carrère, Sybil, and John M. Gottman. 1999. "Predicting Divorce Among Newlyweds from the First Three Minutes of a Marital Conflict Discussion." *Family Process* 38(3): 293–301.

Collins, Nancy L. 1996. "Working Models of Attachment: Implications for Explanation, Emotion, and Behavior." *Journal of Personality and Social Psychology* 71(4): 810–32.

Dana, Deb. 2018. *The Polyvagal Theory in Therapy: Engaging the Rhythm of Regulation*. New York: W. W. Norton and Company.

Ekman, Paul. *Atlas of Emotions*. http://atlasofemotions.org.

Feeney, Judith A., Patricia Noller, and Mary Hanrahan. 1994. "Assessing Adult Attachment." In *Attachment in Adults: Clinical and Developmental Perspectives*, edited by Michael B. Sperling and Willliam H. Berman. New York: Guilford Press.

Germer, Christopher K. 2009. *The Mindful Path to Self-Compassion: Freeing Yourself from Destructive Thoughts and Emotions*. New York: Guilford Press.

Gilbert, Paul. 2020. "Compassion: From Its Evolution to a Psychotherapy." *Frontiers in Psychology* 11: 586161. https://doi.org/10.3389/fpsyg.2020.586161.

Griffin, Dale W., and Kim Bartholomew. 1994. "The Metaphysics of Measurement: The Case of Adult Attachment." In *Advances in Personal Relationships*. Vol. 5, *Attachment Processes in Adulthood*, edited by Kim Bartholomew and Daniel Perlman. London: Jessica Kingsley Publishers.

Hietanen, Jari K., Enrico Glerean, Riitta Hari, and Lauri Nummenmaa. 2016. "Bodily Maps of Emotions Across Child Development." *Developmental Science* 19(6): 1111–18.

Lyubomirsky, Sonja. 2008. *The How of Happiness: A New Approach to Getting the Life You Want.* New York: Penguin Press.

Mikulincer, Mario, Phillip R. Shaver, and Dana Pereg. 2003. "Attachment Theory and Affect Regulation: The Dynamics, Development, and Cognitive Consequences of Attachment-Related Strategies." *Motivation and Emotion* 27(2): 77–102.

Neff, Kristin. 2011. *Self-Compassion: The Proven Power of Being Kind to Yourself.* New York: William Morrow.

Nestor, James. 2020. *Breath: The New Science of a Lost Art.* New York: Riverhead Books.

Porges, Stephen W., and Deb Dana. 2018. *Clinical Applications of the Polyvagal Theory: The Emergence of Polyvagal-Informed Therapies.* New York: W. W. Norton and Company.

Siegel, Daniel J. 2010. *Mindsight: The New Science of Personal Transformation.* New York: Bantam.

Simpson, Jeffry A., W. Steven Rholes, and Dede Phillips. 1996. "Conflict in Close Relationships: An Attachment Perspective." *Journal of Personality and Social Psychology* 71(5): 899–914.

Swann, William B., Jr., P. J. Rentfrow, and J. S. Guinn. 2003. "Self-Verification: The Search for Coherence." In *Handbook of Self and Identity*, edited by Mark R. Leary and June Price Tangney. New York: Guilford Press.

Volynets, Sofia, Enrico Glerean, Jari K. Hietanen, Riitta Hari, and Lauri Nummenmaa. 2020. "Bodily Maps of Emotions Are Culturally Universal." *Emotion* 20(7): 1127–36.

Leslie Becker-Phelps, PhD, is an internationally published author, speaker, and psychologist. She is a trusted expert on relationship issues that people have with themselves, as well as with others. She is author of *Insecure in Love* and *Bouncing Back from Rejection*. She writes the *Making Change* blog for www.psychologytoday.com. In addition, she has created a library of short videos on her YouTube channel to offer people the opportunity to learn how to feel better about themselves and their lives.

Becker-Phelps has a private practice in Basking Ridge, NJ; and is on the medical staff of Robert Wood Johnson University Hospital Somerset, where she previously served as clinical director of women's psychological services, and chief of psychology in the department of psychiatry. She lives with her husband and two sons in Basking Ridge. Find out more about her at www.drbecker-phelps.com.

Foreword writer **Dennis Tirch, PhD**, is founder and director of The Center for Compassion Focused Therapy in New York and the Compassionate Mind Foundation USA. An internationally known expert on compassion-focused psychology, Tirch is author of several books, including *The Compassionate-Mind Guide to Overcoming Anxiety*.

Also by Leslie Becker-Phelps

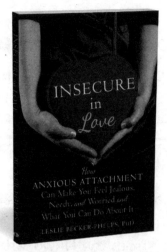

This book will help you get to the root of your
relationship fears and gain the tools needed to
build secure, healthy relationships to last a lifetime.

ISBN 978-1608828159 / US $18.95

This compassionate guide will help you cultivate the resilience
you need to bounce back from rejection—whether it happens in
a romantic relationship, at work, or with friends.

ISBN 978-1684034024 / US $16.95

newharbingerpublications

1-800-748-6273 / newharbinger.com

Did you know there are **free tools** you can download for this book?

Free tools are things like **worksheets, guided meditation exercises**, and **more** that will help you get the most out of your book.

You can download free tools for this book— whether you bought or borrowed it, in any format, from any source—from the New Harbinger website. All you need is a NewHarbinger.com account. Just use the URL provided in this book to view the free tools that are available for it. Then, click on the "download" button for the free tool you want, and follow the prompts that appear to log in to your NewHarbinger.com account and download the material.

You can also save the free tools for this book to your **Free Tools Library** so you can access them again anytime, just by logging in to your account! Just look for this button on the book's free tools page.

+ Save this to my free tools library

If you need help accessing or downloading free tools, visit **newharbinger.com/faq** or contact us at **customerservice@newharbinger.com.**